Routledge Revivals

Authority and Delinquency
in the Modern State

In *Authority and Delinquency in the Modern State*, originally published in 1950, Alex Comfort discusses the relationship between crime and power, and traces the mechanisms which may lead to delinquent behaviour by those in office. In the early twentieth century, the literature of abnormal behaviour contained many hints of identity between the psychogenesis of crime and the psychogenesis of political power, and with the recognition of "war crimes", and the possible criminality of governments, these hints had been brought into the open. His conclusions presented a serious challenge to the traditional conception of Democracy and of the State at the time. He discusses the forces in democratic society which tend to select potential delinquents as candidates for Parliament and for office, or which may operate to produce delinquency in those who obtain power.

Dr Comfort, a Lecturer in Physiology at the London Hospital at the time of publication, obtained his psychological training in child welfare work, but was better known as a novelist and poet. This book was a contribution to the theoretical background of political anarchism which hoped to provoke serious and lively discussion among students of politics and of social psychology at the time.

Authority and Delinquency in the Modern State

A Criminological Approach to the Problem of Power

Alex Comfort

Routledge
Taylor & Francis Group

First published in 1950
by Routledge & Kegan Paul Ltd

This edition first published in 2024 by Routledge
4 Park Square, Milton Park, Abingdon, Oxon, OX14 4RN

and by Routledge
605 Third Avenue, New York, NY 10017

Routledge is an imprint of the Taylor & Francis Group, an informa business

© 1950 Alex Comfort

Publisher's Note
The publisher has gone to great lengths to ensure the quality of this reprint but points out that some imperfections in the original copies may be apparent.

Disclaimer
The publisher has made every effort to trace copyright holders and welcomes correspondence from those they have been unable to contact.

A Library of Congress record exists under LCCN: 51001656

ISBN: 978-1-032-79939-1 (hbk)
ISBN: 978-1-003-49462-1 (ebk)
ISBN: 978-1-032-79940-7 (pbk)

Book DOI 10.4324/9781003494621

ALEX COMFORT

AUTHORITY AND DELINQUENCY IN THE MODERN STATE

A CRIMINOLOGICAL APPROACH
TO THE PROBLEM OF
POWER

ROUTLEDGE AND KEGAN PAUL LTD

first published
by ROUTLEDGE AND KEGAN PAUL LTD.
Broadway House, 68–74 Carter Lane
London, E.C.4
1950

Printed in Great Britain by
Latimer, Trend & Co. Ltd., Plymouth

CONTENTS

v

II THE STATE AND HUMAN BEHAVIOUR

INTRODUCTION

0: 1. In 1948 the Beirut conference of the United Nations Scientific and Cultural Organization initiated a large-scale international research scheme* to provide information on the causes of international and intranational hatreds and tensions. Among the specific objectives was a study of the methods by which Fascism was established, and the causes which might lead to the presence of psychopathic or criminal elements in the government of states.

Psychiatry and social anthropology have not yet existed for a full century as independent disciplines. Within that time they have already brought about a greater revolution in human self-consciousness than any other branch of discovery. The work of Freud and his successors alone has altered our assessment of ourselves at least as radically as did the discovery of evolution. The growth of the idea that the experimental method can be applied directly to matters of human social and individual behaviour has been gradual, however, and much of its revolutionary implication has been masked by this slowness of growth.

Once Western society appreciated the possibilities of the scientific method, it applied scientific investigation to most of its outstanding problems. The nineteenth century saw the beginning of this application to technology and medicine, with results which are familiar to everyone. Conservatism and reluctance were overcome in these fields by the manifest economic and personal advantages, and because, while science profoundly altered patterns of life and behaviour, it did so without the alterations being detected or predicted

* O. Klineberg, *Lancet*, 1949, II, 851.

vii

until they had taken place. Scientific progress brought about the emergence first of the technological middle class, and later of the industrial proletariat. In doing so it laid the foundations of widespread political and social revolution: this process, however, was unrecognized until it was beyond prevention. Moreover the changes were primarily in the distribution of, and competition for, political and economic power, rather than in our estimate of government and society themselves. The basic beliefs of the Chartists and of their opponents concerning the function of government and the methods of altering human conduct were closely similar. Technology gave new resources and new weapons to the established ways of government and industry without calling those methods into question.

Psychiatry developed against this background as an outgrowth of medicine. By the time that it was deliberately called in by institutional society to provide answers to specific problems, such as those of crime, of morale, and of behaviour, it had already grown in its own right to a stature which placed it beyond institutional suppression. Its position in society to-day has been reached largely by its own efforts, and without any conscious attempt to do more than treat sick and maladjusted individuals. Before its full social importance was recognized, even by its practitioners, it had already established principles as full of revolutionary implications for the orthodox tradition of government as those of technology were for the traditional pattern of life.

The Unesco Tensions Project, although it was primarily developed by sociologists, owes its support to the governments represented in UNO. We have here an instance, therefore, of social psychiatry acting under the supervision, and at the invitation of established government. If work of this kind is to continue, it imposes a new type of obligation upon sociologists. The mechanisms of government and the conduct of individuals in authority are a part of the field which is under study, and the exact relationships which can or should exist between modern states and social sciences have never been consciously elaborated by research workers. Something of the kind has been attempted in criminology, the first field where psychiatry was invoked by the State, and there is already a clear-cut split between workers who accept the law and its administration at their face value, and those whose approach is primarily experimental and critical.

It is only within the last few years that psychiatry has been formally invited by legal, administrative and executive authorities to intervene in the problem of crime. It worked its way into penal and legal procedure from the outside, by modifying public opinion and by throwing light on problems of delinquency in the course of purely medical studies, and the formal invitation comes when a generation of lawyers, prison commissioners and legislators has grown up in the intellectual tradition which social studies have created. Psychiatry therefore brings into its contacts with law a tradition of its own, cutting across the preconceptions of law and government which come from the pre-scientific tradition of society.

The attempt to establish criminology as a distinct branch of knowledge encounters immediate difficulties. Anti-social conduct and delinquency, in the sense of action and attitude prejudicial to the welfare of others, are psychiatric entities: crime, on the other hand, is an arbitrary conception embracing both aggressive delinquency, such as murder or rape, and actions whose importance is predominantly administrative, such as the purchase of alcohol after closing time. Since the scope of crime depends directly upon legislation, it may be altered at any time to embrace any pattern of behaviour. Under modern conditions it is quite possible for the criminal psychiatrist to be confronted with the task of reforming an individual whose conflict with society arises from a high rather than a low development of sociality. Refusal to participate in the persecution of a racial minority, or in the military destruction of civilian populations, have recently figured as crimes in civilized Western societies. Under these conditions the independent tradition of the psychiatrist must lead him to decide at what point the psychopathy of the individual exceeds that of society, which he should attempt to fortify, and by what standards. More important perhaps is the growing awareness that, great as is the nuisance-value of the criminal in urban society, the centralized pattern of government is to-day dependent for its continued function upon a supply of individuals whose personalities and attitudes in no way differ from those of admitted psychopathic delinquents. Society, so far from penalizing anti-social behaviour *per se*, selects the forms, often indistinguishable, which it will punish, and the forms which it must foster by virtue of its pattern. The egocentric psychopath who swindles in the financial field is punishable—if his activities are political, he enjoys immunity and esteem, and may take part in the determination of laws.

o: 2. In spite, therefore, of the extent and seriousness of delinquency as a social problem, its most serious aspect for humanity to-day is the prevalence of delinquent action by persons immune from censure, and by established governments. The importation of science into the study of crime is an irreversible step, and its outcome can be only the suppression of science itself or the radical remodelling of our ideas of government and the regulation of behaviour. The present study is an attempt to point some of the morals and speculations which we can draw from existing results. The distrust of scientific workers for the expression of political opinions is well founded, but its maintenance at present is increasingly precarious. Part of this distrust arises from the dangers to scientific integrity when science is applied to emotionally charged subjects in the presence of insufficient fact. Under these conditions the sociologist can only accept the advice of East* to be faithful to scientific standards and earn the respect of his colleagues. But a point must be reached in the near future when the possibility of suspending judgment upon the questions raised by authority, power and government must yield to an accumulating body of fact. We should not com-

* N. East, *Society and the Criminal*, 1949. H.M.S.O., London.

mit ourselves prematurely, but committal cannot be postponed indefinitely by acquiescence in traditional patterns. Social psychology is already invited to give its opinion on issues such as the control of industry by workers and the selection of personnel for positions of responsibility. It can fulfil these assignments only if it is willing to undertake, and has already undertaken, the systematic study in terms of fact of the mechanics of Western political society. This is in no sense the political transformation of science. It is the supersession of the traditional and the empirical in political thought by the same painstaking study of fact which has displaced the empiricism of magic in medicine, and the empiricism of intuition in biology. It is therefore the end and the worthy outcome of a sociology based on reason.

o: 3. The object of this study is to relate the elements in the behaviour of modern governments which lead to the international equivalent of crime to those with which we are already partly familiar in individuals. Society has throughout its history treated crime as something hostile to itself, to be abolished by punishment or prevention. At the same time it has arbitrarily delimited the conduct which is criminal, while depending to a greater or lesser extent on the presence within itself of potential delinquents. No society based on centralized power has been able to dispense with large groups of people whose make-up is in no way different from that of punishable delinquents—it has abolished private, but tolerated public, executioners, for example. Some of these mechanisms will be examined here. While some such toleration has always been present, its study to-day gains urgency from the alarming growth of delinquent acts by states and by organs of power during the last fifty years.

If we are asked to what extent government in modern urban society tends to select psychopaths, and to what extent such selection, if it exists, is responsible for gross social evils or dangers, we can only reply that the experimental evidence is at present inadequate to give a conclusive answer. The social psychology of government is in its infancy, in spite of the responsibilities which are being forced upon it by events. Preliminary studies such as those of Lasswell, Bartlett and others suggest that a case can be made out for the existence of delinquent and potentially delinquent persons in office under democratic societies. A rather stronger case exists for the role of centralization in the production of such behaviour disorders, and for the basically psychopathic character, in terms of certain defined standards of health and normality, of the impulse to secure power and leadership. A case of this kind presented at the present time might call forth an equally convincing refutation. The appeal of its conclusions to other, non-governmental, types of psychopath is an added ground for caution in putting it forward.

It is, however, far too generally assumed by scientific writers on sociology, as well as by the public, that national traditions and 'ways of life' which are, or appear, antagonistic to tyranny and misrule are necessarily free of its defects, or will automatically prevail in spite of the pressure of other forces. The statement of the Nazi leaders that they consciously employed the mechanisms of social democracy in order to subvert it shows deep insight into political realities. The fact that social democracy has advantages by comparison with tyranny does not mean that it, or any other form of centralized authority, must necessarily receive the approval of social studies, once these are applied to the conscious modification of society. It is to advance these problems, by what must at present remain special pleading, that this book has been written.

I
DELINQUENCY
IN MODERN GOVERNMENT

'Even less different from overt criminals are
those latent criminals, high in office, whom
society venerates as its chiefs.'

LOMBROSO

1. GENERAL CONSIDERATIONS

1: 1 *Crime and Delinquency*

CRIME consists in the deliberate violation of a provision which the law upholds by the threat of punishment. Any act or omission which entails a liability to punishment is a crime. 'The great leading rule of criminal law is that nothing is a crime unless it is plainly forbidden by law.'* The limitations and obligations of criminal psychology and psychiatry, as they are applied by administrative penologists, arise from this legal definition, since it prescribes their terms of reference, and casts the net from which their material must be drawn.

Delinquency, on the other hand, is not a conception which the law recognizes. It is, in its present sense, a name given by psychopathologists to those forms of behaviour disorder which manifest themselves in injury to others, or to society.

A clear appreciation of this distinction is essential to any study of the place which delinquent individuals occupy in society. Crime and delinquency would be synonymous only in a society where all forms of anti-social conduct were punishable by law, and where no law prohibiting private, harmless, or beneficial actions had ever been promulgated. In general, the laws of civilized countries claim, and have presumably attempted, to realize such a state of affairs, with the reservation that the law should punish an action only if it harms the community at large, private wrongs being redressed by civil proceedings. Jurists of the last century in this country accepted this as a practicable ideal under conditions

* R. v. Jones: 2 *Ld. Raym.*, p. 1013.

3

of justice and good government. The emphasis of much Continental law at the same time was on comprehensiveness in the code of specific prohibitions, outside the limits of which the individual could not incur legal punishment: law in England was based on a greater reluctance to restrict personal judgment unless and until specific and grave public cause should arise. Penal sanctions in support of better conditions of employment, and against the ill-usage of industrial workers or slaves, were at one time opposed on this ground. Legal utilitarianism gave to the legislature an increased sense of confidence in the power of such specified prohibitions to alter society or to maintain its existing form, and this opposition was gradually overcome.

The idea of crime to-day, however, reflects no accepted system of natural law. Anthropology has shown us marked similarities in the pattern of human standards in several types of culture, but it has also shown us the cultural conditioning of a very large number of the beliefs which determine whether an action shall be regarded as anti-social. Under certain cultural conditions, cannibalism, parricide or infanticide have been regarded not only as innocent but as obligatory. The social attitudes which determine the laws governing offences against the person, property, and sexual ethics antedate by centuries the legal sanction. In communities at a low level of legal development, the sanctions of punishment are replaced or reinforced by the sanction of public disapproval. To a large extent, the older body of criminal law, which existed before the industrial transformation of Western societies and the extension of centralized urban culture, was a law based on the mores—of ruling groups, of the Christian religion, of the cultural tradition of conduct which had grown up in the transition of society since the Middle Ages. The law did not coincide fully with the mores, since it contained elements introduced by rulers to preserve their own position; neither did it coincide with the mores which various pressure-groups desired or attempted to impose on society. A long succession of attempts to bring adultery and fornication

4

within the scope of criminal justice records very vividly the unenforceability of standards at variance with majority practice.*

In so far as the criminal law of pre-industrial societies tended to be a compromise between the ethical standards and the mores of rulers and ruled, some identity was retained, if not between crime and delinquency, at least between crime and socially inacceptable conduct. Eighteenth- and nineteenth-century rationalism and religion both hoped for a continuance of this association. At the present time, we cannot say that these hopes have been realized. On the one hand, the uniform pattern of regional mores decayed with striking rapidity with the growth of predominantly urban cultures—on the other, the centralization of government extended the scope of purely administrative law, supported by criminal sanctions, to the point which it has now reached. The object of this newer law was not the enforcement of the mores, but the maintenance of society, and its maintenance according to the policy and beliefs of the legislators.

We can therefore divide modern crimes into offences against the older mores of property, sexuality and the person, and offences against the policy and methods of the centralized legislators. The standards by which delinquency is judged are personal to the psychopathologist who makes the judgment. For him, delinquency may mean conduct demonstrably prejudicial to others, or conduct which, by its violation of custom and belief, brings the perpetrator into conflict with his environment. The second definition might be held to include many types of eccentricity which have no social content, and is best abandoned. It is clear, however, that delinquency is by no means confined to criminals, or criminality to delinquents. Bentham had long since recognized the existence of 'imaginary offences' which have no social significance beyond that which they acquire from prejudice, mistake or the asceticism of the times. Such offences have existed in all cultures, the attitude of English law to homo-

* G. May: *The Social Control of Sex Expression.* Allen & Unwin, 1930.

sexuality between consenting adults being a case in point. The penal psychiatrist may recognize a case for reconciling such offenders with orthodoxy as a means of relieving their conflicts, even where he and they are convinced of the irrationality of the law. Far more important is the recognition that of two otherwise identical delinquents, both engaging in conduct prejudicial to others, the one may be taken and the other left.

Uniformity of detection and punishment has never existed in human society, and previous cultures have tolerated more and wider economic and political privilege than our own. The powerful swindler, the robber baron, the carnal ecclesiastic and other accepted and honoured delinquents have been a feature of all historical periods. Such individuals readily become the leaders of groups and nations in which their delinquency, like that of an established criminal 'big shot', can be directed against external enemies, very frequently to the benefit of the economic and political status of the group which the delinquent leads. To some extent, too, the power of domestic persecution and misgovernment has been limited by the resources which the tyrant, local or national, had at his disposal, by the resistance of his subjects, or by the competition of others. Primitive societies fall fairly readily into two groups, one conforming to this pattern, with a warlike, predatory and often, though not invariably, tyrannical mode of life, and one in which the direction is predominantly peaceful and social. Family, economic, and cultural factors play a large part in the determination of such group traditions. It is possible in many cases to speak of 'power-centred' and 'life-centred' cultures.

The history of more complex cultures shows a similar behaviour. In the record of unified Western civilizations, both elements are demonstrable, though conventional history devotes more space to the eventful careers of aggressive groups which have moulded political institutions by force than to the cultural and gradual influence of the non-aggressive, which have left their mark mainly by assimilation and

6

influence. Similar patterns also exist within single cultures, but with the growth of centralized authority there is a distinct migration of the two main types of historical delinquent, the potential tyrant and the potential henchman, into the urban society which is the focus of government. Some part of the division between law, the instrument of authority, and the mores, a product of slow development and custom rather than of individual action, may run parallel to the antithesis between City and Court on the one hand and rural societies on the other.

In our own culture, and under the circumstances in which the psychological study of delinquency has grown up, we are dealing with a product of this process which differs from the earlier phases. At the present time, we have to contend less with the delinquent whose success and energy silence opposition than with the widespread incorporation of delinquent patterns of conduct into the actual structure and mechanism of society. Economic and political authority have become coextensive with civilization, and civilization has grown, since the industrial revolution, largely at the expense of the 'life-centred' elements. Law and administration, with their rapid changes in the face of rapidly moving events, and of shifts in the balance of political power, have tended to supersede tradition and mores. The tyrannies which have alarmed and scandalized Western liberalism in recent years have acquired even wider powers of general enforcement than those enjoyed by local chiefs in small communities, because they have been relatively unlimited by custom, and have acquired means of moulding and altering custom and belief on a quite unprecedented scale. We have to recognize that centralized urban cultures, including our own, have come to select in detail the types of individual delinquency, otherwise indistinguishable, which they tolerate or reward on the one hand, and reprobate and punish on the other. The scope of the laws defining crime is no longer strictly limited by the mores of society or of its predominant groups, while society itself, although it feels itself endangered by the

7

growth of individual crime, has come to depend for its existence upon a supply of the very type of citizen from whom criminal actions may be expected. In such a society, there is a tendency for the criminal to be the freelance, the unlicensed delinquent, who has lacked the skill, the luck or the opportunity to express his delinquency within the structure of authority.

1: 2 *The Delinquent as Citizen*

It is the general conclusion of most modern studies that antisocial individuals are manufactured in childhood. If any society finds itself manufacturing them in unusually large numbers, the increase is likely to be traceable to factors in the pattern of community life which act adversely on the family or on the customs of upbringing which parents adopt. At some point, either in childhood or after it, the individual who is handicapped in this way is faced with the problem of his relationship to the rest of society. Some cultures possess higher powers of assimilating these people than others. The assimilative power of our own culture, measured in terms of final adjustment and 'cure', is comparatively low. But by no means all such potential delinquents automatically become enemies of society. Parallel with the difficulty which centralized societies find in readjusting aberrant individuals is their remarkable power of absorbing them unaltered.

The choice facing the delinquent individual is not between fighting society and being remoulded by its customs and mores. It is between finding an outlet for his delinquency which is sanctioned, and one which is not. The chief factor which makes any overt act 'delinquent' is the assertion in it of the right of the actor to behave without regard to others. He may do so by burglary or murder, and take the consequences, or he may find a place in the social pattern which licences him, within certain limits, to make his assertion unchallenged. *The opportunities for this kind of accepted and acceptable delinquency lie almost entirely within the pattern of power.* If delinquents have an obvious social place in such regimes as that of Nazi Germany, they have an indistinguishable place in the pattern of any community where coercion is an accepted part of social institutions. The 'choice' itself is, of course, almost wholly fortuitous. The outlaw is largely made by his opportunities, his contacts, and by the accident of falling foul of the law early in his career. If the subject's behaviour-disorder affects property, he is unlikely to be able to express it in a tolerated form. If it mainly affects personal relationships, he may well be able to do so.

The initial choice once made, the man who finds means of making his antisociality key with society can do so in two ways. If he possesses any capacity to 'take' discipline, there are many occupations in modern society, almost all of them concerned with the executive side of power, which confer a limited licence for the infliction of pain or of arbitrary authority, and these occupations are of a type indispensable to the present pattern of life. Or the abnormal impulse can be nurtured privately until the point is reached at which the individual, as a legislator or a leader of opinion, can himself write it into the life of his culture. *The machinery of power is itself largely a mechanism by which this can take place.*

The most serious problem in modern criminology is, one might justly insist, that of the indispensable and licensed delinquent. The existence of national and individual delinquency of this kind, and the power exerted over national attitudes by psychopaths, is to-day a graver threat to individual security than accepted crime. In some instances, as in the heyday of Chicago gangsterism, or in Nazi Germany, there is a recognizable interchange between the two: in social democracies the public emphasis is on the second, but the major threat to survival lies in the first. This threat extends both to the cultural and economic benefits of centralized society and to the future of science. When, therefore, scientific psychiatry is deliberately invoked, as it is to-day, to deal with individual crime, it must inevitably become widely involved in the study of the non-criminal forms of delinquency upon which patterns of centralized society have

9

come to depend, since both the demand and the supply of delinquents may be held to be products of that society. The convicted criminal represents, to this extent, not so much an eliminable by-product of our culture as a divergent surplus of one of its manufactures.

1: 3 *The Delinquent as an Emotional Outlet*

Beside the function which delinquents and potential delinquents may perform in the institutions of modern societies, they have, in their guise as outlaws and criminals, a second function which may well prove to be even more important. Reiwald* (1949) has drawn attention to the focusing on the criminal and his punishment of a large part of the stray and repressed aggression of civilized publics. He divides crimes into the 'satisfactory' and the 'unsatisfactory'—the 'satisfactory' crime is emotionally loaded, and provides the matter of a huge body of criminal and detective literature: murder, the matter of the detective story, and sexual delinquency, the matter of the Sunday newspaper report, are the chief 'satisfactory' crimes. Embezzlement, fraud, and 'fiddling' of all kinds are emotionally 'unsatisfactory'—they do not chime with any of the more prominent sources of guilt in our own minds. The criminal, especially the 'satisfactory' and more or less atavistic criminal, whose punishment discharges the guilt of the reader and the onlooker, is to this extent 'needed' by society. Reiwald doubts whether modern societies could forgo this particular form of projection without finding others more destructive.

The conservative view of punishment and of the law accepts the purposive and deterrent claims of modern criminal codes at their face value, and in doing so certainly underestimates the ritual and magical elements in the development of public attitudes to crime. Many of the startling discrepancies between the professed intentions of the law and the methods which it adopts are due to survivals of this kind. The lawbreaker in primitive societies has a distinct magical

* P. Reiwald, *Society and its Criminals* (Heinemann, London, 1949).

status. The criminal yields in fact to impulses which most members of his culture entertain in fantasy, and which are a source of guilt. By doing so he offers himself as a sacrificial victim on behalf of the less impulsive or better-repressed members of society, who are duly grateful. In this sense the idea of the condemned man as saviour and exorcist long precedes its use in Christian symbolism. It has been both stated and denied that punishment as we understand it is unknown in most primitive cultures—the execution of a criminal, which may take the form of a suicide, is less a penalty than an exorcism, in the cleansing effect of which the whole of society shares. To this extent the criminal in deed may even be applauded for discharging the office of scapegoat for the criminals in thought.

Primitive residues of this kind are unquestionably present in modern law, though they are not always easy to disentangle. Reiwald points to the practice which persisted until the last century in England of disguising the condemned man as an animal (by wrapping him in a cow-hide) and the tendency of civilized states to treat trials and executions as a form of festival. Even the medicine-hat which the modern judge places upon his head to pronounce sentence of death has a long and distinguished anthropological history. The interested, admiring, or orgiastic attitude of the public towards its legal enemies is as least as ambivalent as that of any primitive culture. Such links with the criminal as public benefactor establish a possible clue to another form of tolerated delinquency, that of the exacting or tyrannical primitive king. He, like the condemned man, is a magical figure, to whom license is permitted, and who is slain for the ritual benefits of the whole community at the end of his term of office. The king and the condemned wrongdoer are, at some points in social history, interchangeable. The transition from king-slaying to government seems to have been by way of a stage at which the understudy executed in the king's place was, in fact, a condemned lawbreaker. In the words of Reiwald, 'the criminal seeks an unrestrained instinctual satisfaction without regard for the community. Exactly the same trait characterizes the tribal father. It is his position that the criminal, who disregards the social taboos, seeks to assume—and for this reason the unconscious can ascribe to him such an exalted significance.'

Apart from any analytical or historical considerations, it seems fairly clear that in modern centralized cultures the law-breaker and the ruler do in fact occupy opposite ends of a single emotional axis. Both are scapegoats for the undeclared aggressions of the individual: both receive a detectable measure of toleration in the discomforts and injuries which they may inflict on the community by virtue of their office. Reiwald's suggestion that some part of the attitude of societies toward crime arises from a need to maintain it, and to achieve an emotional discharge by punishing it, seems well founded. In the case of oppressive rulers the whole process is more conscious. The toleration of a tyrant, in spite of his inflictions, has often arisen from the fact that he provides a focus for aggressive fantasies in the public, whether they identify themselves with him or react by hatred toward him. Democratic governments, like criminals in democratic societies, also serve as public scapegoats. The rulers relieve us of our dissatisfactions with our irresponsibility, while the punishment of the criminals and the disapproval which we display for them discharge our uneasiness at impulses which we share with the murderer or the sexual offender. Without a great deal more factual knowledge, it is unwise to press conceptions of this kind too far, but modern work on psychosymbolism, and the history of the interplay between the king-victim and the criminal-victim, are too suggestive to be wholly ignored. From the viewpoint of society, the two functions may converge. From their own viewpoint as individuals, ruler and criminal may represent the division between those who seek to express aggression in defiance of society, accepting the punishment which that involves, and sometimes actively, if unconsciously, desiring it; and those who seek to express similar aggressive impulses by becoming themselves the controllers or the conscience-keepers of society, and moulding it to their own pattern.

1: 4 *The Forms of Tolerated Delinquency*

Tolerated delinquents appear in centralized cultures at two distinct levels. They may enter and control the machinery of legislative and political power, as policy-makers and rulers. They may also be found, and tend in general to be more numerous, in the machinery of enforcement which intervenes between the policy-maker and the citizen. We owe our present recognition of the presence and the role of these tolerated delinquents, and of their capacity for mischief, to the rise of totalitarian states, but the reappearance of delinquency and military tyranny as socially accepted policies in civilized states has led, and must lead, to a scrutiny of similar mechanisms within the social democracies.

Social democracy was devised, in so far as it arose as a consciously determined system, to limit the possible abuse of power by delegates. The powers of the delegates themselves were created by public discontent with irresponsible government. In terms of liberal theory, therefore, social democracy should contain extensive safeguards against the capture of authority by delinquent individuals or groups. The Constitution of the United States was framed with this object deliberately in view. The safeguards provided by constitutions and by theories of government, however, leave out of account the far greater effects upon society of economic and social forces which the theorists were in no position to foresee. Democracy is exposed to the hazards which other societies have faced, from the ambition of energetic and unscrupulous individuals, and from the over-concentration of power, but it carries risks of its own. The range of aspirants to political power in a monarchy is limited to the circle of military leaders and the nobility, who might hope for success as usurpers: the wider the qualification for office, the greater the competition. Democratic societies, especially in their centralized form, offer the prospect of entry into public

13

affairs to many aggressive personalities whose ambitions might otherwise be limited to local affairs. The actual control, moreover, which the delegate rulers exercise over the life of ordinary citizens, is more effective and thorough than that which older monarchs could contemplate, and the fact of delegacy limits to some extent the resistance of the public to such control. With the growth of urban society, and the extension of the range and scope of administration, the policy-makers have acquired resources of force and persuasion which meet with very little organized resistance, except in times of economic slump or widespread poverty.

At the same time, the concentration of populations and of political functions in cities has led to a gradual increase in the size and extent of the machinery of enforcement. These organizations gradually acquire an autonomous function, which may be free from the control of the policy-makers and of the public alike. The urban police have played a considerable part in the conflicts surrounding political parties, and in the setting-up of dictatorships. It may be recalled that the Roman Constitution imposed special and deliberate checks on the use of the army for domestic enforcement by the distinction which it drew between *imperium domi* and *imperium militiae*, military commanders being normally divested of authority within the city limits.* The unique sequence of psychopathic emperors who figure in later Roman history owed their power in almost every case to independent action by the enforcement units of the army (the Imperial bodyguard), who were often recruited from, or supported by, foreign mercenaries. In this case the executive was physically and literally an out-group, foreign to the mores and attitudes of Roman society. The breakdown of this system followed upon the appearance in the executive of aspirants powerful and ambitious enough to dismember between them the central authority.

Meanwhile the liberal theory of Western democracies has exercised little or no influence over the pattern of their

* J. E. Sandys, *A Companion to Latin Studies* (C.U.P., 1929).

14

biological growth. Centralization has produced major changes, many of them detrimental, in the status of the family and in the security of the individual, which have not been neutralized by technical advances. Halliday* has drawn attention to the growing importance of culturally inherent anxiety in such societies. The historical evidence drawn from the fate of older city-cultures which have outrun their biological foundations is far from reassuring. An increasing tendency for fear, insecurity, and an orientation towards war to become permanent features of such cultures can be identified in our own. Mumford† has already presented an alarmingly realistic picture of the processes of disintegration in urban aggregates—under these conditions, psychopathic processes and attitudes become pandemic: guilt and its projections in military aggression may become even more prominent in democratic and traditionally pacific cultures than in others which have fewer scruples. The effects of the atomic bomb upon the modern American conscience have been more marked than those of military defeat upon the German. The liberal safeguards in modern social democracy are increasingly forced to contend with factors which never entered the heads of their inventors. The totalitarianisms which modern liberals denounce, and upon which they frequently project their own guilt and insecurity, are the end-product of similar processes in cultures whose resistance has been lowered by tradition or circumstance.

In the aristocratic oligarchies, the personnel of government was recruited by inheritance within the ruling caste, and received occasional accessions from below through inter-marriage and the appearance of new and self-made noblemen. Government was one function among many which this class discharged. In centralized democracies, government is an occupation, and one which generally excludes other forms of activity. It must therefore compete with other occupations of equal dignity and status for the personnel which it

* J. Halliday, *Lancet*, 10th August 1946.
† L. Mumford, *The Culture of Cities*, Secker & Warburg, 1938.

requires. The leadership of a modern political party offers neither economic nor intellectual incentives which are superior to those provided by technology, the professions, or the higher administrative grades of the Civil Services—its appeal to a given individual is likely to depend chiefly upon the power of modifying the lives of others which it confers. The machinery of enforcement, the police and the prison services, has in the past maintained its recruitment because of the degree of personal security associated with government employment. The police and the army were for many years the only pensionable and established occupations to which working men could readily find an entry.* This is no longer the case. The increase of social security and the rise in industrial living standards have largely nullified their appeal. By comparison with other employments, the enforcement services offer poor remuneration and a severer discipline. Here, as in the legislature, deliberate choice is likely to play an increasing part in recruitment. There is, therefore, in centralized societies, a tendency for the personnel of these occupations to be drawn increasingly from those whose main preoccupation is a desire for authority, for powers of control and of direction over others. In the case of would-be politicians, these impulses may spring from a highly developed political and social sense; they may equally well spring from maladjustment and a deep-seated impulse toward self-assertion and dominance. In social democracies there is interposed between the individual who desires office, and the office which he desires, the mechanism of election and of the party system, involving the need to induce large electorates of varying intelligence to support the candidate at the polls. In such a process, integrity and altruism may be at a disadvantage beside astuteness and single-minded ambition. Moreover, while altruism and social idealism may find ready outlets in other fields, such as scientific research, medicine,

* In pre-war England, 70 per cent of prison officials were recruited from the Armed Forces. (*Rep. H.M. Prison Commiss.*, 1939–41.) Presumably the majority of these were ex-regulars.

16

religion, or social service, all of which carry a satisfactory intellectual and social prestige, the centralization of power attracts inevitably towards the administrative centre those for whom power is an end in itself. The desire for success through riches or success through fame and esteem are more adequately catered for in other spheres of society, and though political power may be approached by these other routes it remains the predominant attribute of government in modern urban cultures.

Considerations of this kind may be held to constitute a risk rather than a fact in the psychology of English politics at the present time. The number of ambitious and unscrupulous men in any contemporary parliament is probably no higher than in previous periods when a different background existed. Other factors, however, beside those of party politics may at any time intervene to bring into office, through electoral channels, psychopathic persons or groups who will exhibit delinquent behaviour, either as a long-sought aim, as the focus and expression of pent-up public anxiety and frustration, or through the deteriorating influence which wide power, isolation, and crisis may exert over unstable individuals. The standards of British Members of Parliament, and of the public, underwent recognizable change during the inter-war depression, and during the second World War. Against such changes, and against the stress imposed by modern government upon initially social individuals, institutional safeguards are not likely to prove effective.

Moreover, whatever we may consider to be the normal standard of private integrity, and however fully this standard is upheld by English politicians, a distinct division exists between private qualities and public policy. It is characteristic of political psychopathy to-day that grossly delinquent public policies may coexist with good private adjustment. The suggestion that those who order public frauds, massacres or deportations must necessarily be criminal or sadistic in their private relationships has no support in theory or in observation. Where actions are recognizably psychopathic,

17

the normality of their perpetrators in other fields is not more relevant than the superficial adjustment which criminals frequently display outside their specific behaviour disorder. It seems clear that the intense strain and the other incidentals of modern political office have an observable effect in evoking delinquent conduct in persons who would probably not otherwise exhibit it. It is arguable whether Hitler would have been actively delinquent had he failed to secure office, in spite of his manifestly abnormal make-up.

In discussing these phenomena in their contemporary context, reference may be made to history, but obvious reasons prevent the publication of case-histories or estimates of living persons. The long-range diagnosis of mental abnormality, in a person who is known only through his reported utterances, is in any case to be discouraged. But we can hardly fail to see the relevance of psychiatric classification to the political scene of the last twenty years. The fact that abnormal persons exist, and acquire power, within the political system is not in itself a condemnation of the system. The same applies to other fields of activity. The important judgments upon which we must base our estimate of the modern state are, first, whether it attracts psychopaths selectively; second, whether the impulse to power is itself a manifestation of delinquency, in some or all of those who display it; and third, whether institutional patterns increase and foster abnormal emphases in the state-holders. To answer these questions we must consider the problem from its other aspect, and examine the types of leadership which exist in modern democracies, and their compatibility with stable and social attitudes.

2. TYPES OF LEADERSHIP

2: 1 *Leadership and Dominance*

In relatively simple groupings, the forms of leadership associated with political activity are indistinguishable from those which occur in other fields. They are of the stuff of all human relationships in which individuals, drawing upon their experience and their self-estimate, adopt attitudes of dominance or subservience to one another. The individual's estimate of his own reserves of physical and mental energy continually modify the status which he claims, and shape the body of experience which, in turn, determines his future conduct. These primitive patterns are probably continuous with the type of social dominance which exists in animals.

Antisocial behaviour disorders occasionally occur among normally social animals, especially in captivity. 'Serious injuries as a result of fighting are rare. Occasionally one may meet a rogue mouse who will bite all other males in a cage and inflict serious injury. The others never seem to retaliate, and the rogue may be recognized by the fact that he is the only mouse uninjured. . . . The rogue is better killed.'*

In highly centralized communities, the acquisition of political power depends upon factors other than those which determine purely social hierarchy. Centralized government calls for specialized attributes, and many, if not all, of the elements which fit a man for leadership in a local group retain greater force in fitting him for executive than for legislative office under the party system. There has been a

---

* P. A. Gorer and P. J. Ewers in A. N. Worden's *The Care and Management of Laboratory Animals* (Bailliere, Tindall, & Cox, London, 1949).

profound division and delegation of functions in the city community, with a corresponding limitation of individual aspiration to one, or possibly a few, of many patterns of dominance. Only certain types of intellectual power manifest themselves in political success, the others being absorbed by technology, art, learning, the professions, and education. Physical superiority is a greater asset to the athlete, the entertainer, or the officer of enforcement than to the politician. Special training, a potent factor in occupational choice and success, plays little part in determining the outcome of elections, and the hereditary ruling class has been displaced.

It seems reasonable to assume that while the types of leadership-criterion which are used in the selection of army officers or key personnel are similar to those which determine power and status in simple groups, they are no longer the factors which predominantly affect the choice of governments. Government in urban communities is a group in itself—the legislators influence one another by personal contacts, but the normal factors of dynamic psychology, which regulate status in ordinary relationships, do not apply to the process of election by remote control. They depend upon contact, physical impressions, and personal interaction. The legislature tends to become one of a number of closed groups, having individual dynamic relationships within itself, but interacting with the electorate chiefly through mechanical channels of publicity.

This relationship, or lack of relationship, is one of the fundamental realities of centralized government. The rulers and the ruled have their own group hierarchies, but the relations of the public with its government are those of a group facing a stereotype, and the relations of the government with its public are those of a group facing a crowd. This crowd may be the physical audience of the mass-meeting, the dictator's rally, and the conference, or the fragmented crowd which listens individually to the radio, or reads individually the statements in the press. In the first case, the older patterns of leadership retain a hold, reinforced by the myth of leadership—in the second, the individual faces not superior individuals but an out-group, detached from the group of neighbours or colleagues which makes up his own dynamic orbit. The criteria of psychological and biological leadership may be valid in a military unit, a neighbourhood, or a factory, but they are not transmissible by wire or in print. The problem of attaining dominance becomes one of creating the illusion of these attributes, an illusion which may readily be destroyed if governor and governed once meet at the personal level—the politician may be compared with the actor who, from a wheel chair or a sanatorium bed, impersonates the man of action, the soap-opera hero, and is invested by radio listeners with his physical attributes. Such techniques offer a ready appeal to those who must simulate that which they do not possess. The individual who possesses concrete leadership-attributes expresses them in fields where only the reality is adequate: he is the sub-leader, the executive front which protects the mythical leader from personal contacts by which his leadership may be tested. Political leadership in large unitary organizations is essentially leadership untested by the dynamic contacts which determine dominance within the group.

Studies of leadership in modern societies may deal with one of these two patterns, or a confusion of both. Leaders have been classified as crowd-representatives, crowd-compellers, and crowd-exponents (Conway) or as institutional, dominant and persuasive (Bartlett). These categories are rather techniques of leadership, one or all of which may be employed by individuals within the group, or by governments facing their public. The institutional leader, like the biologically forceful individual, is probably predominant in the executive, though in other capacities: the dominant is present in executive and legislature—the more able he is to withstand the tests of personal contact, the more likely he is to favour the executive side of government: the persuasive, who replaces impact by the power of 'selling himself', is a conspicuous feature of democratic political life. Totalitarianism imposes other emphases, but its pattern appears to be similar.

It is possible to infer that so long as political units are small, that politics is not an exclusive occupation, and that personal contacts between ruler and ruled exist at the normal level of dynamic psychology, leadership attributes of the type recognized by psychometric tests will predominate in determining status within any pattern of privilege which exists. Where government is a largely autonomous function, carried on by whole-time politicians, where the size of the political unit exceeds a limiting value, and where precedence does not depend upon face-to-face contact, the 'natural' leader is at a distinct disadvantage compared with the candidate who possesses the ambitions rather than the attributes of leadership. Histrionic power, access to technical aids and expert advice, and deliberate or accidental canalization of crowd feeling are far more significant in determining office than the ability to command, to inspire confidence at the personal level, or to gain a reputation for foresight.

2: 2 *Physical Attributes*

Physical characteristics figure largely in the normal mechanisms of dominance, since they play a large part in determining initial impressions, and may dictate the attitude of their possessor as well as his fellows. Associations have been made out between small stature and aggressiveness, between height and selection as leader; there are obvious correlations between appearance and physical energy. Considerations of this kind influenced the early criminological approach to 'degenerate' types. In studies such as that of Gowin* differences of stature, though not very great between various groups 'suggest that in certain types of leadership and headship, involving physical powers, height and weight are important in determining dominance roles'.† Physical attri-

* E. B. Gowin, 1915.
† Kimball Young, *Handbook of Social Psychology*, Routledge & Kegan Paul, 1946.

butes such as a beard, which are measures of oneness with, or foreignness from, communal custom, may influence employers against an individual, and even predispose him to crime,* while to the criminal who requires to evade recognition, certain types of physical peculiarity are serious occupational handicaps.†

Personal attractiveness and physique may play a large part in influencing meetings and committees. Under modern conditions, they are less significant electoral characteristics than are idiosyncrasies. The democratic politician's needs are almost the full opposite of the criminal's—he must secure ready recognition. Even the malice of cartoonist opponents is a valuable source of publicity. It is difficult to conceive Mr. Neville Chamberlain without his umbrella, Mr. Eden without his hat, or Mr. Churchill without his cigar and his individualities of pronunciation. The public appeal of Mr. Morrison, Mr. Bevin and Sir Stafford Cripps in the present Labour administration has been enhanced by the readiness with which they can be caricatured, by their opponents no less than their supporters. The political leader who wishes to hold the public imagination may be tall or short, thin or fat, but he must be memorable—he cannot afford to require a written label in press cartoons. With the advent of radio, and the possibility of direct verbal approach to mass electorates, voice and delivery become even more important. Reputations have, in the last few months, been seriously damaged overnight by an unconvincing and pedestrian delivery. In contradistinction to the mass meeting, the broadcast discriminates against rhetoric—the audience is at the wrong emotional pitch to receive it—and against overeducated speech, which may be identified with snobbery or officialism. Regional speech, moderate idiosyncracy, and a power to convey the impression of admitting the audience to inner confidences without condescension, play an in-

* H. von Hentig, *The Criminal and His Victim*, Yale University Press, 1948: citing P. V. Young, *The Pilgrims of Russian Town*, 1932.
† Ibid.

23

creasing part in the maintenance of politicians in public affection. With a change in public temper such techniques may be rapidly superseded—the 'family chat' would have been as inept to the Germany of 1930 as the ravings of Hitler would be to a modern English audience. Voice to this extent supersedes physique and appearance as a source of initial reaction —it may, in common with the printed word, produce an illusion which can be overturned by an injudicious personal appearance. Stalin is reported to have written of his first meeting with Lenin:

> I had hoped to see the mountain eagle of our party, the great man, great physically as well as politically. I had fancied Lenin as a giant, stately and imposing. How great was my disappointment to see a most ordinary-looking man, below average height, in no way, literally in no way, distinguishable from ordinary mortals.*

The political leader in centralized orders can, in short, only afford to risk the tests imposed by other forms of social dominance and personal contact if he possesses characteristics which have general psychical validity, and which can surpass the average as his public knows it—otherwise he will fail, however masterful he is, to fulfil the expectations which prestige has built up. He must be able to surpass not the best men in a limited group, but the collected best men of a number of groups, of large extent and wide variety. He must impress Jew and Gentile, bond and free, man and woman, sufficiently to secure their votes, and much may be gained or lost by initial impressions. Under these conditions the tendency to withdraw behind a pretorian guard, into the use of techniques which permit sophistication, or into the study of current and irrational public sentiment for openings, is well-nigh irresistible. 'All cameras corrupt: television cameras corrupt absolutely.' The natural leader can find scope for his talents in an active group life—the individual who has the taste rather than the qualifications for leadership can find compensations for what he lacks only in

* Isaac Deutscher, *Stalin*, 1949.

24

the centralized method of government and promotion.

2: 3 *Leadership in the Executive*

The size of the executive in centralized societies makes it hard to differentiate from other groups, such as finance and productive industry, into which it overlaps. In the United States, where industry is in private hands, the executive in Government employment has been estimated to include between 4 and 10 per cent of the employed population. Most of this staff is employed in organization and the keeping of records. Mumford has emphasized the increasing expenditure of time in urban societies upon the keeping of documentary records and accounts, and the large number of people withdrawn from creative and productive activity may contribute to the 'increasing frustration of creative and biological impulses' mentioned by Halliday as a source of psycho-social neurosis,* although leisure occupations and cultural interests compensate for some of the drawbacks of clerical work. The effects of such specialization must, however, play some part in determining the behaviour of a culture in which it is so widespread—executive clerical workers in business and government make up a significant electoral group, second only in numbers to industrial and technical workers.

Apart from this electoral function, the most important executive groups, from the standpoint of governmental structure, are the *professional administrators*, the *agents of public information*, and the *agents of enforcement*. These groups tend, as we have seen, to act as buffers between legislators and electorate. At the same time, they retain a considerable policy-initiative of their own. Kimball Young† distinguishes between the higher policy-making civil servant, who may resemble the legislator rather than the lower executive officer, and the subordinate, for whom the main attractions of public service are order, routine, and security rather than direct initiative.

* Halliday, J., 1946. op. cit.
† Op. cit.

Like the enforcement agencies, the institutional Civil Service and the information agencies intervene between legislator and electorate. The former is a hierarchy of its own, demanding certain definite characteristics—its highest members, who may not have passed through the lower ranks of the machine, resemble the legislators in function, although they are free of direct electoral responsibility. Their position as implementers of policy blunts, to some extent, the competitive side of their contacts with the actual legislator, who is at a disadvantage through ignorance of the detailed administrative mechanism. They do not, therefore, compete directly for national leadership, though they may become objects of substantial jealousy in the eyes of their responsible ministers. This interplay of personality-types has been better worked out in fiction* than in formal psychological studies.

The information agencies are of greater importance, since they are the main means by which the elected legislator addresses his public. In these agencies public prejudice and attitude are both represented and deliberately modified.

The object of issuing information from any such ministry is, of course, the same as the object of 'writing up' a patent medicine. It is to *select* favourable news and present it accordingly.... With the lowered morality which Grotius observed as characteristic of warfare, the selection of information may of course amount to a selection with intent to defraud.... What is not so generally realized is that originally, and often persistently, most main currents of propaganda are believed by their authors to be essentially and in substance true.

In individuals, subnormal standards of veracity are often accompanied by persuasive eloquence of tongue or pen. Men with such equipment have early made the discovery that for them truth-telling is not essential to happiness. And such men may find themselves in the exercise of their talents either upon the political stage or in remunerative journalism. The machinery of political propaganda may be influenced, or even directed and fed, by men of such character. Probably it often is. But these men seldom initiate policy. They are the possessors of arts which minister to the convictions of

* Nigel Balchin, *The Small Back Room*, 1945, for example.

26

others. The initiators of trends of political propaganda are men honestly and profoundly convinced of the need of their mission, however wrong-headed or fantastic that mission may seem to others.*

The enormous expansion of salesmanship in modern societies has its political component. The idea of the 'collaborator' as a wartime phenomenon has no basis in fact—collaboration, in the derogatory sense, may originate in a masochistic delight in defeat, but a large part of it is the wartime counterpart of the normal executive status. The salesman, concerned with the technique of selling rather than the merit of the article sold, already occupies a definite place in the pattern of administration.

Extensive American studies of the chief motivating 'drives' in consumers and of the optimal psychological make-up of the salesman could be transferred bodily to the field of political advertisement. During and since the war, professional advertising consultants have been increasingly employed to 'sell' policies. The control of literary and artistic patronage by government agencies may extend this executive function into art, fiction, the film, and the Press. In totalitarian orders such control rapidly becomes absolute: in our own, both official and independent patronage coexist, and no decisive financial hardship attached to dissident literary work, even in wartime. The Press can, and does, act in some circumstances to palliate or hinder delinquent policies by making them public—Emerson was partly justified in describing demagogic democracy as 'the government of bullies tempered by editors'. The democratic politician has, however, come to rely very largely on presentation by advertising. He may even come to rely upon theatrical stage-management, make-up, and elocution-training, which enable him to compete with professional actors and broadcasters before a critical audience.

2: 4 *Incentives in Politics—Politics as a Condemned Occupation*

Prestige in society has always been a strong incentive to

* Ranyard West, *Conscience and Society*, Methuen, 1942.

seek political office. It appears that this is less true to-day. In fact, there are signs that the disrepute attaching to politicians in ancient China and in modern France is more prevalent now than it has ever been in this country.

Most societies have regarded certain occupations as disreputable, even if necessary. Branches of the enforcement-executive have often fallen under a cloud of this kind. The ancient rabbis classed tax-gatherers as robbers,* together with ass-drivers, barbers, sailors, and shopkeepers. The prestige of the professional army fell in much the same way during the early years of the present century. Trades whose practice was supposed to make men immoral (actors, singers, dancers), effeminate (weavers, who pursued a feminine occupation), dishonest (millers—who, under feudalism, enjoyed rights from the lords of the manor which made them highly unpopular) or which involved killing (butchers, and even fishermen) have been similarly disapproved at various times, and their practitioners incurred disabilities.† Hangmen have always been the prime example of a condemned occupation. The acceptance of the office of hangman at most periods of history must have implied either poverty or a morbid personal inclination.‡

While it would be far-fetched to detect so strong a condemnation of politics in the modern public, the sentiment that party government is a matter for sharps, and politics a 'dirty business', has a limited but definite existence to-day. It may readily turn to abuse of a particular party, or take the form of apathy rather than distaste (what can one man do against the system?)—but French opinion since the Stavisky scandal, and to a lesser extent American opinion during the period of Tammany Hall and the political czars, have been sufficiently hostile to politics, as an occupation, for honest men to think twice before standing for office. English

* *Jewish Encyclopedia*, XII, 69.
† For references see H. von Hentig, op. cit.
‡ See the brilliant development of this theme in a modern context by Arnold Zweig, *The Axe of Wandsbeck*.

28

political life has been safeguarded from the worst suspicions by its freedom from direct financial bribery: the most marked anti-political feeling is probably that of demobilized armies looking for a scapegoat.

> Grim fusiliers broke ranks,
> Snapping their bayonets on to charge the mob,
> At last the boys had found a cushy job.
> I heard the Yellow Pressmen grunt and squeal,
> And with my trusty bombers turned and went
> To clear those Junkers out of Parliament.*

The prestige-element fades considerably from political life when attitudes of this kind become widespread. They may result in a gradual diversion of intelligence out of politics into other fields of endeavour, or they may be passed on as father-to-son advice. Clever or popular governments can do much to rehabilitate themselves, as the New Deal rehabilitated American politics, but a scandal or a disappointment can easily reverse the position. The most surprising feature of this disillusionment is the rarity with which it expresses itself as positive action or direct disobedience.

It is clearly a matter of great importance in any sociological study of modern government to assess the motives which actually lead individuals to stand for office. The incentives which political life offers no longer include wealth or the prestige of former times. An individual is likely, therefore, to become a candidate either because he has a strong social sense and a desire to end abuses and benefit his country, or because he desires power and its satisfactions and has failed to achieve them through the normal mechanism of dominance. In some cases the incentives are separate, in others they may merge, or the ideology may be a rationalized excuse for the ambition. Strong public convictions may in themselves be a product of abnormality: few leaders can have surpassed Adolf Hitler in their sense of mission. Others may desire power as a vehicle for revenge (upon the system which left

* Siegfried Sassoon.

29

them with family memories of the Means Test—upon the society which declined to give them the social recognition they desired) or from the prohibition-complex which leads to the foundation of societies for the prevention of something. Not all these attitudes are either abnormal or in the long run harmful—societies progress through their least contented members. The centralized system of election, however, selects very heavily against the principled and the moderate, and against those leadership-attributes which de-depend on face-to-face contacts. The best adjusted members of most parties occupy the back benches rather than the Ministerial front bench. The rational leader may ultimately have a decreasing chance against the determined climber and the psychopath who reflects the attitude of the frustrated crowd, or who is living down his own failures of adjustment.

Political power offers superb platforms to the unconscious play-actor from childhood—to shout defiance at erstwhile school-fellows whose hands are no longer able to reach out and twist his arm, to prove the prizeman in yet one more test, to hurl yet more fiends down to hell before the final reckoning comes, to scoff at still more nannies and greybeards.*

* Ranyard West, *Psychology and World Order* (Penguin Books, 1945).

3. ABERRANT PERSONALITIES IN GOVERNMENT

3: 1 *Character Structure*

THE form of the legislative House and its traditions are more important safeguards against psychopathic individuals than the electorate. It would be extremely difficult for a grossly insane or deluded Member to conceal his mental state under the conditions of Commons debate—parliamentary methods also provide a restricted field for the testing of personal qualities, which is probably as searching as any aptitude or leadership test. The Hitler-like abnormal has therefore a far better chance of doing mischief in the executive than in the legislature, so long as this system endures. Congress, lacking the close intimacy of the Commons, is a less searching test—legislatures with no tradition of orderly debate provide none whatever. In assessing the kinds of mental disturbance which may pass unrecognized in politics, and the risks they present, we have to allow for the type of legislature concerned. It has to be remembered that even severe disorder is not always recognizable if its exterior is amiable. The non-political delinquent faces, and often solves, the problem of keeping up appearances under conditions of everyday life. The greatest psychological hazards of parliamentary democracy are prejudices, the desire for violence or for suffering, and situation-neuroses sufficiently deep-seated in the personality to appear only under stress, and accompanied by plausibility or force of character. Decisions taken in private, or personally, as under war conditions, are the most likely to be tainted with such attitudes, occurring in personalities which would probably be adequate in any ordinary context of power—the damage comes from the enormous repercussions which such decisions, made by a minister of a modern state, may have.*

The executive imposes severer tests on the entrant, but gives less protection against abnormality once status is attained. Provided the subject performs his functions, he is unlikely to be ejected on grounds of personal peculiarity. The executive can also advise the government in an expert capacity, and thereby disarm criticism. A considerable number of war crimes have originated in pressure from the executive, often from a single member, backed by expert assurance that they were necessary, even though deplorable. Manifestly psychopathic generals may be strikingly successful with their troops†—equally psychopathic police officials may achieve great credit for their assiduity in punishing crime and maintaining the law. Wherever the conscience of legislators tends to run counter to the course forced on them by 'realism', the executive is apt to be left to its own devices and enjoined to do what is needed without undue publicity, and by a process of the same kind the doubtful task is re-delegated within the executive to its least scrupulous member. Few members of parliament who support capital punishment would wish the criminal to be hanged from their own door-knocker—even fewer would wish to be involved in the military policies which they vote as regrettable necessities. We all exhibit a tendency to sit 'with a clothes-

* 'The acceptance of genocide as a national "military" policy . . . was made under pressure of war, without public debate of any kind; and it was the work not of moral cretins like Hitler and Goering . . . but of men as conscientious and upright as Secretary Henry L. Stimson. . . . Even to-day a full sense of what was involved in this decision has not, apparently, struck home to any large part of our (American) citizens.' Lewis Mumford (*World Review*, 1949, 9, 14: *The Moral Implications of the Atom Bomb*.)

† General Patton's celebrated address to his troops, reprinted by the American magazine *Politics* (1945), is a psychological document of extreme interest: unfortunately its phraseology and content make it impossible to quote the text.

pin in our noses to keep out the stink of the processes which keep us alive'.* The legislature, moreover, is often ignorant of the exact physical details of the policies it is voting.

Any classification of public delinquency must include most, if not all, of the known manifestations of behaviour-disorder, since delinquent behaviour may arise in a wide variety of conditions. It is increasingly recognized† that by no means all delinquents, and still less all criminals, can be recognized as mentally abnormal. The 'non-sane, non-insane' individual is our greatest problem. Some definite patterns of imbalance are, however, particularly common sources of anti-social behaviour. Organic psychoses, because of their slow onset in previously normal persons, readily acquire social importance—schizophrenia, in its extremer forms, is unlikely to be compatible with political activity, though it may occur in religious or quasi-religious prophets who exert a wide influence. Manic-depressive psychoses are compatible with active and influential participation in public life—they may impair judgment, especially in their milder forms, without being recognized by the patient or his colleagues, and cyclical depression in high places has been stated to have caused the failure of campaigns. Paranoid, hysterical and obsessional patterns may also have obvious public import-ance: most significant, however, in terms of modern politics, are the varieties of psychopathic personality, not amounting to psychosis, and certain of the neuroses. Even the high grade mental defective, since he is the ideal henchman, and the 'moral defective', if well-preserved, tend to occupy charac-teristic positions in the structure of society.

The *inadequate psychopath*, while he may drift into crime, is less likely to drift into office, since drifting is an unsatis-factory means of preferment in a competitive society. Where he acquires responsibility, as the neutral third between agres-sive opponents who cancel one another out, as may occur in Trade Union or National elections, he may achieve some

* George Orwell.
† Norwood East, *Society and the Criminal*, H.M.S.O., 1949.

popularity as a facile, genial, and superficially sociable character, whose placidity and emotional blunting can be mistaken for profundity. Unable to cope with crises or unpleasantness among colleagues, on whom he depends, and by whom he may be flattered, he may react to emergency by frenzied efforts to establish control, or by the aggression of the cornered rabbit. A few such characters have passed across the political stage in recent years, and their survival-time in democratic orders is probably longer than in tyrannical, since they lack the predictability of the sound henchman.

The aggressive egocentric is a far more typical figure in the political struggle. The antisociality of these subjects is as much a matter of attitude as of overt behaviour—they are conceited, ambitious, domineering and intolerant.

It is not merely a question of degree which here separates the normal from the abnormal, but the fact that emotional instability and an inability to profit from experience make the conduct of the aggressive egocentric psychopathic personality incalculable, unreliable and often dangerous. The qualities which require firm guidance if success is to be attained are uncontrolled and act injuriously to the man as well as to society.*

The individuals of this type who possess a measure of control and a good intelligence gravitate easily into positions of dominance—they are the inherent bosses, for whom the status of unchallenged leader is a major end in life. Other cases may be predominantly acquisitive, and reach positions of responsibility in business, provided that their carelessness and their uncritical estimate of their own powers do not involve them in trouble. The advent of a totalitarian order extends enormously the range of disordered behaviour of this type which is compatible with high public office—the egocentric who can conform sufficiently to a higher and more successful egocentric is likely to be valued for his bluntness, absence of sentimentality, and aggressive attitude toward inferiors.

* Norwood East, op. cit., 1949.

34

Ethical aberrant personalities, characterized by a complete absence, or severe impairment, of moral responsibility, which may go with acute intelligence and a superficially rational and plausible exterior, make dangerous and determined criminals, but tend in general to act alone,* and are more likely to emerge as political figures on the crest of a wave of revolutionary violence than through the normal channels of election; mere disregard of moral standards is not a sufficient cause to include an individual in this group, and the genuine moral imbecile is apparently uncommon. Some at least are the result of organic psychosis—others have been regarded as constitutionally abnormal.† Cases have occurred where such persons have attained hereditary or even elective office—the Emperor Caligula has been so diagnosed by some workers.

Of these types, the aggressive and acquisitive are by far the most likely to scheme for, and attain, high office. The extent to which they are able to do so will depend upon the pattern of society. During the early phases of industrialism, the predominantly acquisitive psychopath found ready scope in the expansion of industry, commerce and finance. His emergence was, in fact, the signal for the passing first of laws designed to safeguard his financial victims and later of laws controlling the conditions of industrial employment. To this extent the increased opportunity for acquisitive delinquency in centralized societies has hastened the extension of political control. Changes in institutions, and in the economic position of Britain, have already greatly reduced this opportunity. Determined delinquents of the acquisitive type probably find a more congenial outlet in crime or near-crime, and the financial rewards of politics are not likely to attract them. Where, however, as is usually the case, financial success is a means rather than an end in itself, and its pursuit is motivated by the desire to enjoy the power and security which accompanies wealth, a book-keeping estimate may be

* Norwood East, op. cit.
† D. K. Henderson and R. D. Gillespie, *Textbook of Psychiatry,* 1944.

35

inadequate. Power in its totalitarian form has been seen to provide adequate rewards both to vanity and to avarice— Goering's medals and his collection of pictures belonged properly to the search for ostentation rather than to the acquisitiveness of the miser. Acquisition *for its own sake* is probably a relatively uncommon form of delinquency.

In postwar English society, psychopaths of the power-acquisitive type are probably likely to flourish on the fringes of government, as contact-men and wire-pullers, rather than within it as legislators. In America, the earlier pattern of business competition remains, and the egocentric psychopath has provided the model of a widespread national myth of success. By virtue of their hero-status, such individuals can intervene in politics to safeguard their interests or gratify their ambitions with greater ease than in Britain, where they command a less reverent public attitude.

The other main offender against property derives at least as much satisfaction from the use of his wits as from the rewards they bring him. The centralization of urban democracy has brought the techniques of electoral propaganda and those of commercial advertising into very close proximity.* While greed is unlikely to propel an individual into Parliament, where his income may actually be reduced, and his opportunities of adding to it curtailed, the confidence-man is as much a figure of urban social-democracy as he is of underworld society. In rural communities the confidence trick is of necessity the stock-in-trade of the itinerant rogue. It can only become a sedentary occupation in large social aggregates, which provide both concealment and a supply of victims. The confidence man is more dependent upon his victim than any other type of criminal—he can operate only if he has access to the credulous, the acquisitive, the bewildered, and the insecure. These characteristics are prominent in the urban electorate: while it is upon credulity and

* For an illuminating short account of the applied psychology of advertising and advertisers, see M. A. Blosser in J. S. Gray's *Psychology in Human Affairs* (McGraw Hill, New York, 1946.).

greed that the criminal swindler depends for a livelihood, his political counterpart depends largely upon the existence of a sense of insecurity, and the desire of the public to appoint a trusted delegate. Of the elections in Britain between 1918 and 1940, at least four were decided by means which closely resemble those of the criminal trickster. These included the spreading of rumours affecting the security of savings, the forgery of documents, which were then released to influence public opinion, and the promise of direct financial gain. From the psychiatric side, a similar parallel has been noted.

Although there are many habitual criminals who specialize in using the mails to defraud, there are many others who have been convicted of this offence who are not essentially different in their psychological make-up from the average candidate for public office. The promises of over-sanguine inventors, mining-stock promoters, and a large number of brokers are of the same timbre as those of candidates for Congress or Governor who secure votes on the strength of promises they can never fulfil.*

A desire for personal violence finds little direct outlet in the activities of modern democratic legislators. In primitive aggressive societies, dominance passes readily to those who possess strength, initiative, unscrupulous determination, and self-confidence. Of such material were the majority of successful and unsuccessful usurpers. The ascendancy of such individuals has a number of parallels in animal societies. In domestic poultry† and among mice in captivity there is evidence that dominance depends on hormonal factors, and an individual can rise in the social hierarchy as a result of injections. One effect of centralization has been to remove these biologically potent and dominant individuals from the legislative to the executive side of society. The opportunities for purely physical displays of initiative, or for the gratification of a love of personal violence, must be strictly limited

* J. G. Wilson, and M. J. Pescor, *Problems of Prison Psychiatry*, p. 71. 1939.

† W. C. Allee, *Science*, No. 95, p. 289. 1942. W. C. Allee and N. Collins, *Endocrinology*, No. 27, p. 87. 1940.

for cabinet ministers. National military leaders at the legislative level are increasingly non-combatant civilians, and events such as the Siege of Sidney Street are increasingly the province of the police or the army. Where a preoccupation with violence exists in civilian legislators, it is more likely to be of the fantasy type, the realization of which, in genocide, indiscriminate warfare, or persecution, is if anything more serious to society than the behaviour of the individual bully. The enforcement machinery, however, together with the armed forces, is still the sole socially legitimate outlet for aggressive physical adventure.

This relationship too, under democratic conditions, has been appreciated from the psychiatric side. The high occupational incidence of crime in American police officers mentioned by a number of criminologists is not evident in England, and must be set against their contact with the underworld, their opportunities and temptations, and the need for realism in law-enforcement which makes the maintenance of a quasi-criminal fringe by the police inevitable. The selection of occupations in which violence is necessary or tolerated may, however, be a mark of the delinquent.

The police force and the ranks of prison officers attract many aberrant characters because they afford legal channels for pain-inflicting, power-wielding behaviour, and because these very positions confer upon their holders a large degree of immunity; this in turn causes psychopathic dispositions to grow more and more disorganized. . . . It is wrong to limit the group (*of moral imbeciles*) to the criminal. It is often forgotten that many of our legitimate vocations require a lack of emotional sensibility. Prototypes are the executioner, or the officer who applies the lash to a prisoner. Yet these are only the crassest instances, those which cannot be smoothly concealed behind the screen of means justified by the end.*

In the case of women prison officers the correlation is possibly even closer.† The terminal phase of such a process may perhaps be found in the records of the Belsen trial.

* H. von Hentig, *The Criminal and His Victim*, 1948.
† F. Monahan, cited by H. von Hentig, ibid.

Both in the modern prison system in this country and, pre-eminently, in concentration camps, active delinquents are readily recruited to the enforcement machine as 'trusties'.*

The desire for violence and for the infliction of pain or of destruction finds its expression in modern government through the fantasy-delinquent, who seeks office as a means of realizing his fantasy, or who, once in office, succumbs to opportunity and rationalization; and in practice among the personnel of war and of enforcement. Among the fantasy-aggressors, another factor may play a part. Such destructive impulses not infrequently coincide with, or are projections of, an inner psychical conflict which may involve a deep sense of guilt, and their realization in practice, however rationalized, may accentuate that guilt. A certain number of persons, among them many whose instability expresses itself in ambition, may manifest such guilt as a profound unconscious desire for punishment. Flügel† has produced strong arguments for the existence of such a desire, which may be present even in those whose social conduct and uprightness do not lead them to expect punishment at the hands of society. While punishment in prison or otherwise fulfils such a need in the criminal delinquent, it is not necessarily a final relief of his conflict, any more than the repetition of any other neurotic compulsion relieves the underlying neurosis: in the non-criminal or non-delinquent legislator, however, it may conceivably precipitate decisions of a catastrophic and pain-producing kind, in which the individual and the society which he governs are punished together. The deep sense of aggression and guilt underlying much of the behaviour of Nazi leaders may partly explain the attraction for them of a total and irrevocable Götterdämmerung. Forces of a similar kind may also play a part in determining the choice of war-

---

* E. Lingens-Reiner, *Prisoners of Fear*, Gollancz, 1949; R. Phillips (editor) *The Belsen Trial* (War Crimes Trials) Depositions, 1949; W. McCartney *Walls Have Mouths*, Gollancz, 1936.

† J. C. Flügel, *Man: Morals and Society*, 1945.

or of national subjection by less obviously psychopathic political leaders.

The fantasy-delinquent has found a new field in the executive services which devised and handled wartime propaganda. Atrocity propaganda, in the form of derogatory and horrifying accounts of a group enemy, and of his misdeeds, has been found in all cultures: in its modern form, which has already come to play a large part in war and in peacetime political campaigning, the technique of atrocity propaganda is highly stylized. It consists in recounting horrific, and especially sadistic, happenings, which may be true or false, but which are presented primarily in a form which evokes sexual stimulation rather than simple fear or distaste. This stimulation of repressed responses gives rise to a sensation of guilt rather than of disapproval, and the guilty thought is then projected against the public enemy. A study of most of this propaganda, and of the public response to it, shows fascination and desire to be as strong components of its effectiveness as civilized anger at barbarity. Atrocity propaganda plays a considerable suggestive part in the production of certain types of delinquency, both in civilians and in armies. A number of the fantasies of the first World War, such as the 'corpse factory'* were actually realized by the combatants of the second World War.

Paranoid psychotics, and pre-psychotics, occupy a special position in centralized politics, because their tendency to project their grievances against external bodies, such as racial minorities, institutions, and nations strikes a deep chord of sympathy in the minds of anxious and frustrated electorates. The pre-paranoid may be indistinguishable from the over-emphatic grumbler: how far he is likely to attain office will depend on the direction in which he systematizes his resentment. Should he project it against a body such as the Jews or the police, he may become the centre of a pogrom or a riot: if his imaginary enemies have more than a local validity as figures of fear and dislike, he may go far. The

* E. Ponsonby, *Falsehood in Wartime*, 1936.

paranoid shows a marked tendency to discuss his opinions, to conduct propaganda for them, and to acquire adherents. Most instances of *folie à deux* represent the sharing of a paranoid grudge. This process is helped by the gradualness with which the delusion goes beyond the bounds of reason, by the skill with which it may be argued, by the presence of a basis of original fact in most cases, and by the walling-off of the abnormal part of the mind from other fields of mental activity. In politics, paranoids who attain office early are particularly dangerous, since they often become more and more deluded with age, and the public and their colleagues may grow up with their prejudices on a basis of toleration. Strictly paranoid attitudes towards the Jews, the Communists and the Germans have been observable in democratic statesmen of our own time, quite apart from public projections of resentment against these groups.

It is fairly obvious that extreme paranoiacs are unlikely to be acceptable members of parties which pursue policies based on self-interest or social objectives, or in the more disciplined revolutionary parties. They may, in some cases, be used, since their preoccupation gives a handle to any astute colleague who desires to manipulate them. Mild paranoid symptoms are, however, not uncommon in aggressive psychopaths, since they spring naturally from the resistance of society to the impact of these people, and this dangerous combination has accounted for some of the most serious anti-social actions by governments.

An elderly company promoter who had held Cabinet office in one of the Dominion Governments was charged with murder. His immediate history before the crime had included a bankruptcy and a libel action, but he had no criminal record, and his sanity was not suspect. It appeared in the course of the trial that he had suborned two thugs to decoy and murder a young man of whom he was jealous, the jealousy being in regard to a middle-aged woman whom the victim had met three times only. No defence of insanity was advanced, but subsequent psychiatric examination revealed a whole system of insane delusions, some of them of long standing. In political and business life the man had been rude, forceful, overbearing and suspicious, but he had apparently been accepted by his colleagues. During his trial he remained confident, resourceful, and perfectly able to organize his defence, as he had done the crime.

The interest of this case lies in the extent of the unrecognized mental disorder. Had this man remained in politics, and reached high office, or had his paranoid ideas taken a turn against a national rather than a personal enemy, his mental state might never have been called in question.

Addictive psychopathics have from time to time played a part in politics. The Nazi hierarchy is stated to have contained several morphinists. Alcoholism, since it is the only addiction tolerated by society in spite of marked effects on performance and social behaviour, is also the only important addictive factor in the discussion of English politics. During the eighteenth and early nineteenth century, drunkenness among legislators was part of a more general social toleration, which diminished greatly as the century progressed. At the present time the use of alcohol among legislators is probably not different from its use among higher business executives. Public drunkenness to the point of incapacity is hardly tolerated, though it has occurred, but from the standpoint of government the association of entertainment on a lavish scale with diplomacy retains considerable importance. In the highly charged atmosphere of international manœuvre, alcohol may be both a deliberate weapon and an accidental influence. The modern man in a responsible, and often overburdening, situation uses alcohol as a source of relief where his eighteenth-century counterpart used it as a source of conviviality. Careers cut short by alcoholism are far from rare in democratic politics. Both the over-conscientious and the over-convivial may contract it: in many cases the emphasis is less on personal instability than upon the enormously increased stresses of centralized government, of which the egocentric and the cynical are less likely to be aware. Alcoholism may therefore prove a means of weeding out the more conscientious legislators. It also offers peculiar risks to the successful left-wing representative who cannot stand up to calculatedly lavish hospitality. Persistent moderate alcoholism, because it is undetected, likely to affect the over-conscientious, and most pronounced in times of crisis, is the manifestation of addiction which is most likely to exert a direct influence on public affairs. Among the enforcement personnel, alcohol plays an important part in switching individual conduct from tolerated to non-tolerated forms of aggression, in occupation armies, *élite* troops, and occasionally the police. The elements of control which enable a psychopath to keep his behaviour within the tolerated pattern are the first to succumb to intoxication.

Other delinquent patterns. The delinquencies tolerated in war will be considered separately, since war is by far the most important psychopathic activity of modern states. It is important to realize, however, the tendency which modern centralized governments appear to exhibit toward the permanent war economy—in the face of external enemies, as a natural expression of public attitudes, and the projection of guilt and resentment, which may be deliberately focused on out-groups in order to divert it from revolutionary channels, and as a reaction to economic pressure. War is the condition in which centralized government finds itself most fully in control, most secure in its authority, and most readily able to command undisputed public allegiance. The unity of purpose, real or fictitious, which results from defence or attack is as intoxicating experience for authority as it is for a public which is weary of the isolation and aimlessness of urban asociality. For such societies war may be a release of guilt and tension. It is their finest hour. The more marked the tendency to incorporate war methods and war attitudes into peacetime life, the greater the demand for civic and subordinate psychopaths. The wartime demand for individuals willing to stab in the back, to dissemble, to forge, and to seduce enemy agents, has its peacetime parallel. The personnel of espionage, and possibly also the research and

43

technical staffs who devote themselves deliberately to the elaboration of mass destruction, fall into this category. The degree of psychopathy present will depend on the extent to which such people act under the influence of a systematized dual standard, of responsibility at home and aggression towards the permitted enemy, and the extent to which their choice of employment is the result of factors in their previous personality. Under conditions of 'cold war' the paranoid individual, employed as a propagandist, may also acquire importance—his mood is in key with the general suspicion and tension.

3: 2 Gangsterism

The term 'political gangsterism' is, generally speaking, an inaccurate description of social delinquency in its modern context. Gangsterism in its observable form bears little relationship to the pattern of government. The majority of studies of American gangs show them to resemble predatory primitive societies, following some at least of the normal dynamic patterns of leadership, though modified by interchange with the society upon which they prey. 'Each gang, in turn, is stratified; the boss lives by the standards his admirers and followers put on him. He must comply with their expectations—it is better for him to be a dead lion than a live dog.'* The relations of gangsters with government and enforcement in the United States show that this exchange with the environment operates in both directions. Interactions between gangsterism and politics were also occasionally noticeable in the rise of the Nazi party and in resistance movements, such as the Maquisards and the I.R.A. Protection of well-organized gangs by law officers, and their intrusion into local and national elections, have been a product of local conditions in the United States which have never been reproduced in England.

Gangsters generally enter into the pattern of tolerated delinquency, if at all, by virtue of their status as individual

*H. von Hentig, op. cit.

aggressive delinquents, rather than as organized bodies, and in doing so they commonly transfer allegiance to the State and away from the gang. It is more accurate to say that enforcement agencies and dishonest or violent political activities divert into themselves individuals who might otherwise have expressed their abnormality in organized crime. The social forces which produce gangsters also produce social delinquents. Like the gangsters who, in Chicago, bought their way into office to further the activities of the gang, these potential gangsters may secure a dangerous degree of protection from institutional law, but the criminal intruding in politics is, by the obviously unacceptable character of his activities, in a far less secure position.

The equation of fascism or Nazi-ism with organized crime has, therefore, an element of truth, but little psychological value. The gangster is a delinquent who accepts or creates organization to help him, but who remains a publicly inacceptable delinquent. His hostility to society limits his incorporation into any but its crudest delinquent activities. He may buy power, or secure it in his capacity as a hired exponent of violence, but the established régime relies on its own enforcement machinery, and his scope is limited to the provision of a rival machine which may be used by revolutionary or paracriminal parties. If he enters such a body early and rises to power with it, his position is identical with that of the institutional 'strong-arm' man. Gangsterism in social democracies is an alternative to the State—in totalitarian orders it appears to be absorbed by the State, or to be practised by dissidents who have fallen from the institutional machine.

3: 3 The Investigation of Governing Groups

So far we have discussed factors which may be expected to operate in modern government. An investigation of the extent to which they do in fact affect our own society is clearly necessary before the speculations themselves can be accepted. The evidence which we have used is drawn from a great many sources, but there is so far no authoritative study of the personalities of governing individuals, on which we can rely, or which is at all comparable with the large number of studies of criminal or mentally deranged delinquents.

The practical difficulties of verifying any hypothesis about the criminology of power are particularly forbidding. It is relatively easy to study the mentality of any type of delinquent other than the delinquent in office. Lawbreakers in prison, or psychiatric cases referred to clinics, provide material for study which is either relatively docile or relatively defenceless. As penal psychiatry has repeatedly found out to its cost, no proper estimate of the forces behind conduct can be obtained by studying the actions of the accused, the court records, or even the delinquent's account of himself, unless these are supplemented by interview, and preferably by prolonged personal study. Personal study is, however, one source of information about modern political and executive leaders which the form of society to-day effectively limits. The criminal delinquent, moreover, is usually either unidentifiable from his case-history, or is convicted and sentenced, whereupon the psychiatrist can cite his case without serious risk of legal consequences. With the politician, it is not only inadequate to base long-range guesses about motivation upon public utterances or policies, but any imputation of abnormality would be unlikely to fall within the legal definition of privilege or public interest. For this reason I have been forced to avoid documenting this study from contemporary events. The only full and quotable data concern the Nazi war leaders, who were admittedly psychopathic to a degree which limits the use of the records drawn from their trials in discussing less deranged societies. It would be quite unjustified to draw unlimited conclusions about politics in England from the conduct of an exceptionally psychopathic regime. It is possible that in America, where anonymity can more easily be preserved in dealing with a more numerous and diverse group of rulers, and where libel is differently construed, sociologists might find it easier to document their work.

At least one serious attempt to study the relationship of abnormality to political leadership has been announced in connection with the UNESCO Tensions Project. The Beirut Conference instructed this Project 'to study and report on the techniques and devices used to bring about Fascism in Italy and Germany . . . in order to assist the early recognition of such movements in the future . . .' and recommended 'that the results of this study should receive wide publicity'. Work is also announced 'from which we hope to learn about the way in which leaders in different countries have risen to important positions, and how some individuals get to be leaders who are later diagnosed as psychopathic'.* The results of this work, political and scientific, may prove to be important, although scope and methods have not yet been announced.

* O. Klineberg, *Lancet*, 1949, II 851.

4. WAR AND THE CORPS D'ÉLITE

4: 1 Sociology of War

Wᴀʀ is by far the most important type of group-delin-quency in contemporary societies. It is both an institution and a psychopathological entity, but at the present time it has come to assume a permanence in urban centralized cultures which cuts across its institutional history. As a pattern of sustained aggression and resistance against a foreign, execrated group it has assumed a permanent place in ways of life and techniques of government in these cultures. It has come to fulfil the definition which a French cartoonist attributed to the Prussian military catechism:

> What is peace?
> Peace is the period of preparation for war.

Warlike cultures have always existed within historical times, but their attacks on their neighbours were largely dictated by short-term advantage, such as spoil, empire, or the gratification of national pride. From the standpoint of the individual in the tradition of his culture

individual aggressiveness stems from early interactions, associated with either personal-social or cultural conditioning, and the institutions of war may offer a person an outlet for aggressive motives built up in the early years.*

While these elements still influence national aggressiveness, they have been supplemented, if not superseded, by the importance which centralized living gives to war as a means

* Kimball Young, op. cit., p. 340.

of government. To the individual whose incentives have been gradually pared away by delegation, and who can no longer compete for leadership or proficiency in a circumscribed group, aimlessness and lack of status are continual anxieties. Describing the source of psychosomatic disease in modern England, Halliday* relates the growth of anxiety to

increasing separation from outward roots in earth: increasing disregard of biological patterns; increasing frustration of manipulative creativity; increasing rapidity of change in society; increasing standardization and repression of individual expression; decreasing sense of aim and direction.

and continues:

Only, perhaps, in wartime, and under inspiring leadership did the masses regain some sense of purpose and direction.

The big city and the large, convenient administrative group impose solitariness, and reduce the variety of social activities which the individual can undertake for and in himself, at least as much as they increase the total scope of experience. The amateur musician who could compete with his friends cannot compete with the lumped resources and talent of professional entertainment. Something analogous takes place in social dominance-patterns. War is the only surviving national activity in which the opportunity to shine is combined with a full indulgence for aggressive behaviour and a pressing invitation to the individual to participate. Almost all other communal activities take place through a chain of delegation so long that its end is lost to the sight of the individual—only in war are *his* effort and *his* capacity appreciated: no delegation interposes between the soldier and the enemy, or between the civilian public and its appointed tasks of 'staying put' or 'going to it'. The sense of purpose and unity which war artificially creates are, for urban cultures, a drug of addiction. Regarded with fear, it

* J. Halliday, *Lancet*, 10th August 1946.

may be accepted with relief and seen in retrospect with regret. It provides a personal experience both of emotional release and of social cohesion which may outweigh its horrors. Huge operations are conducted by god-like and infallible leaders, for objects expressed in perpetually repeated and readily understood stereotypes. Emotion and excitement based on physical fear and physical aggression are kept at a high pitch—the violence of the film, the gladiatorial show and the suicide motor race, standard addictions of asocial cultures which provide a more limited release for aggressive desires, cannot compete with the violence of war. Problems can be shelved and replaced by action or by appropriate gestures. The atmosphere of the nursery, with its securities and insecurities, of being in the hands of those who know best, is recreated. The genuine fear and hatred of war under these conditions cannot disguise its satisfactions. The citizen is placed in the same situation toward forbidden acts of aggression as the child who is suddenly given the run of the forbidden room, or the repressed adolescent who suddenly gets access to sexual satisfaction. After such an orgy, return to reality is as painful as continuance in danger.

This ambivalence makes the threat of war and the promise of war two of the most important political forces of our age. They react with equal force on the legislators. War, consciously or unconsciously, is for them a suspension of difficulties and of conflicts—so long as it continues, demands and agitations cease to be dangerous, confidence and solidarity can be maintained, opposition can be identified with the enemy, and the dramatic aspect of public actions is increased beyond all peacetime precedent. It provides a distortion of reality in which abnormal impulses may pass as normal, and irrational ideas achieve unquestioning acceptance. It simplifies power and administration to a series of undisputed attitudes.

It is essentially the socially maladjusted civilian who is happiest in wartime—his problems are shelved, the difficulties of his personal relationships are superseded: the criminal can redeem himself by enlisting his delinquency on the popular side: the paranoiac is at grips with an enemy whom others beside himself recognize and revile. The adjusted individual finds his entire life disorganized, his family broken up, his liberty curtailed and his protests regarded as treasonable. War is essentially the playground of the psychopath in society. The intermediate majority experience both aspects of war, and in societies like our own, which traditionally condemn personal violence, guilt as a reaction to war is widespread. The majority of participants accept the oversimplified version of the issues, often after severe mental struggle, because they see no alternative—they fail, however, to accept the institution or its implications. The public which acclaims victories cannot be allowed to see over-realistic films of commando training, or its morale will suffer. A fiction of controlled, discriminate violence has to be maintained, and is readily destroyed. The wartime government is always perplexed by the difficulty of assuring, in democratic orders, that resolution or exhilaration does not turn to disgust, and in totalitarian orders, that the emotions aroused do not recoil in aggressive resistance to the arousers. The democratic war administration has to lead a horse to the battle without allowing it to smell too much blood—the dictator has to ensure that the lynch mob does not lynch the instigators as well as, or instead of, the victims.

Revolutionary movements subsist by projecting social evils, including war, upon the ruling group—given a change of institutions, war will vanish. Governments may employ the same methods—war is identified with Hitler or Napoleon, or with a nation or group, and the defeat of this enemy is the road to permanent peace. Sociology has rightly stressed the function of war as a meeting-point for aggressive impulses in society as a whole, and the importance of stereotypy, projection, group myths, hostility to foreigners, and individual aggressiveness. While the war-orientation of modern societies is unquestionably the outcome of such factors, it would be unrealistic to minimize the role of governments. In fact, few if any of the more disastrously delinquent acts of nations in recent years are, in the final analysis, the result of spontaneous upsurgings of public aggression. The attitude of the centralized society towards war is always ambivalent, but the manifestations of warlike tendencies are predominantly under the control of governments. Neither the German extermination of Jews, nor the Allied massacre of enemy civilian populations, which have been cited as the two most widespread and serious group-delinquent manifestations of the second World War, were spontaneous. In the case of the Jews, spontaneous feeling was inflamed, intensified, and artificially maintained by a legislative group: in the case of the policy of indiscriminate bombardment, intensive propaganda failed to still all public doubts of its necessity and morality.* Elaborate public rationalization of both actions took place through official channels of information. Public sentiment against war is and was traditionally strong in Britain and America, and was by no means absent in Germany. Elaborate trickery was in many instances required to reconcile public opinion to participation—allegations have been made that the Pearl Harbour incident was manipulated in this manner, and the change in American public opinion between 1940 and 1941 was unquestionably due in part to active governmental pressure. A marked exception was the forcing of war upon the British Government in 1939 by a spontaneous public reaction, which had as its origin widespread suspicion of complicity between British right wing thought and the Nazi ideology.

If contemporary wars were in substance, as well as in background, the direct expression of aggressions projected from the urban public as a whole, we should not expect to find any such elaborate rationalizations as Hitler, or we ourselves, employed, except as a means of allaying the guilt of those

---

* A Gallup Poll in May 1941 showed only a 53-38 per cent majority in favour of indiscriminate bombing as a reprisal—these figures showed a strong positive correlation between experience of air raids and disapproval of reprisals. (Reported, *News Chronicle*, May 2nd, 1941.).

who offer them. While the revolutionary overestimates the role of scheming diplomats, the sociologist may readily underrate the part played by governments, and individuals within them. The replacement of Hitler by another less paranoid leader, even an exponent of the same ideology, might have produced a marked change in the pattern of history. In assessing the causation of war, it is impossible to overlook the part played by conscious choice, by economic activities such as those of armament firms and financial 'lobbies', and the deliberate use of war as a means of government by diversion.

With the exception of such activities as looting or the sack of occupied territories, wartime delinquencies and 'war crimes' do, in fact, originate more commonly in specific individual delinquency among the ruling groups than in crowd behaviour. Crowd manifestations such as those of the early days of the Franco-Prussian War have been relatively uncommon even in totalitarian countries without deliberate stage management. Their main consequences have been limited delinquency such as the ill-treatment of prisoners, lynchings, or simple civil crime. Abundant evidence exists that a large part of the fighting and civilian populations retain intact the majority of their civilized attitudes towards their fellow-men in any instance where there is direct contact.* In the case of the Japanese, much of the barbarity exhibited toward prisoners belonged to a cultural tradition wholly unlike that of Western Europe, and was no greater than the barbarity of discipline existing within the military group itself. The most reprehensible acts of the second World War were almost all committed either upon superior orders, or by *élite* enforcement bodies, selected by institutional rulers, and indoctrinated to perform them. In some cases, the authority derives from a leader of the crowd-exponent type, and the psychology of such actions closely resembles

* Impressive evidence on this point is provided by the quotations collected by Catlin, *et al.* (G. Catlin, V. Brittain and S. Hodges, *Above All Nations* (Gollancz, London, 1945).

that which has been studied in the peacetime lynch-mob. In others, delinquency is the planned execution of a pattern of individual fantasy.

There is documentary evidence relating most of the calculated and indiscriminate war crimes to the invention and planning of individual psychopaths in office. The role of group projection and stereotypy is greatest in producing acquiescence at the lower levels of the chain of command. In some instances, the effective lack of hand-to-hand contact assists this process—few regular fighting men would have accepted an order to massacre civilians in detail, by means involving contact, but many were capable of acquiescence in forms of indiscriminate war which did not destroy the stereotype or upset the security of the rationalization.* In other cases, acquiescence was limited to non-participant consent, while the actual deeds were performed in private by the selected *élite*, part of whose function was to perpetuate public acquiescence by terrorism.

In our own society, the fighting man and the public commonly take the view that the element of personal risk amounts to an atonement for specific delinquency. It is only after five or six years that one can criticize, say, indiscriminate air bombardment, without evoking violent hostility from those who point to the heroism and the severe losses of the air forces concerned. If the extermination of the Jews by the Gestapo had involved any element of personal risk at all comparable with the hazards of action, it is doubtful whether any marked public indignation could have been aroused. English reaction, especially among bombed civilians, was far greater and more hostile when attacks were carried out by pilotless flying bombs than when orthodox bombs were dropped by vulnerable air crews. Primitive expiatory ideas of this kind play a notable part in maintaining acquiescence in democratic countries. Individual pacifists have been known to abandon deep-seated rational or unconsciously motivated attitudes in order to share the hazards of a war

* A. T. Harris, *Bomber Offensive* (Collins, London, 1947).

54

which they disapproved—others deliberately courted punishment or discomfort to maintain their self-respect in the company of serving soldiers. The extreme apprehension which the atomic bomb has produced in England and America is almost certainly due to some such expiatory sentiment, rationalized as a fear of physical consequences. There appears to be a difference in kind between the reaction of the Russians, whom the bomb may have been intended to intimidate, and that of its makers, whom it has succeeded in intimidating beyond all reason.

During the second World War, psychiatry as a science was brought into direct contact with these problems, since it was invoked as a deliberate weapon, to select military personnel, to advise on morale, and to devise means of demoralizing the enemy. 'The military psychologist is not obligated to theorize about causes of war. He is one element in society's cutting edge concerned with the most effective prosecution of the war, and must operate on the assumption that war is, or will be, a *fait accompli*. . . . In the conduct of psychological warfare, the psychologist need not attempt to cultivate new distrusts . . . : instead, he merely selects existing fears and purposes. In any nation he has only to fan certain flames and smother others to make the fire burn where he wants it.'* Psychiatry is practised by human beings, who share in the attitudes of their time—it has also a rational discipline of its own. It was, in general, considerably more at ease in demoralizing the enemy by exposing his irrationalities than in co-operating with the group policy. The question of standards of normality became acute—the degree of cultural acceptance of war as an institution is to some extent reflected in the tendency of German military medicine to study the total personality of the officer candidate, while that of American psychiatry was to select specific aptitudes. Whether psychological methods were ever applied consciously to the selection of extermination squads or

* G. L. Fahey and M. M. Mintz in J. S. Gray's *Psychology in Human Affairs* (McGraw Hill, New York, 1946).

prison camp guards is not known—aptitude selection in these groups seems to have taken place within the structure of the Nazi party. In general, the traits of the good officer in either army, despite the allegations of pacifists, were closely similar to those of the social leader in other categories of life. Civilian armies lack the intense group psychopathic traits of wartime civilian populations—they make up a community of shared danger, where status is determined by simple rules, and where much of the isolation and stress of centralized civilian life is broken down. The last war produced many examples of what have been termed 'paraprimitive' groups, based on comradeship and common undertaking, in which normal differences of rank were obscured. The sense of responsibility which the officer felt for the lives of his men is something conspicuously lacking in civilian political hierarchies. Few if any political leaders could write with sincerity

> Because to love is terrible, we prefer
> the freedom of our crimes . . . *

A feature of this tendency, reflected again and again in the growth of private languages and common phraseology, is the increased splitting-off of the civilian soldier from the civilian. The soldier sees himself as alternately defender, scapegoat, and victim of the home public and the home administration. Total war, by imposing a less violent contrast between groups than that between England in the first World War and the trenches of Flanders, has slightly reduced this tendency, but it retains a good deal of political importance in creating a discontented block vote, and in determining change of government at the end of hostilities.

There is nothing in the study of the modern civilian army to suggest that it is primarily either a delinquent or a brutalized group at the social level. The most serious effects of military service appear to be on sexual and family attitudes, the damage being reflected rather in the next generation than in those who undergo it, although these too

* F. T. Prince, *Soldiers Bathing*.

56

experience serious difficulty in adjustment. Commanders of such armies have in general experienced more difficulty in preventing fraternization than in preventing outbursts of individually prompted aggression. Highly politicized armies may be regarded as belonging to the enforcement-*élite*, but they, too, readily lose some at least of their stereotypes when actually in contact with enemy populations. A sustained hostile occupation of relatively unaggressive territory presents serious administrative difficulties to the high command. It rapidly produces assimilation, sexual encounters, bridging of the gap between victor and vanquished, and loss of fighting spirit. *Francs-tireurs* and resistance movements, while they undermine immediate morale by creating tension and confusion, may, to this extent, actually facilitate the psychological task of the occupying power.

It will be seen from these considerations that the aggressive energies of frustrated civilizations and persons are responsible for wartime delinquency far more by enabling psychopaths to secure office and obedience than through direct outbursts of violence. '*La terreur d'aujourdhui a ses bureaux*,'* and the individual citizen contributes to it chiefly by obedience and lack of conscious or effective protest. Social obedience and conformity are, in general, rather less prominent in centralized urban than in primitive or in civilized rural communities. The urban community retains and conforms to its own mores, but these are neither so well knit nor so universally respected as in other types of society: those which concern social and political attitudes have been widely modified by rapid change in living, and are increasingly external to the individual. The primitive man tends in general to conform actively—the civilized urban citizen combines an acquiescent attitude towards the executive with an apathy toward public standards which expresses itself either in cynicism or in a conviction that 'they' (the legislative group and its executive fringe) cannot be effectively resisted by his own efforts. Obedience towards the law at

* Albert Camus.

57

the same time lacks the active features we find in societies where law and mores coincide. The delinquent is less and less regarded with personal animosity—the non-conforming individual, even when grossly criminal, has a tinge of hero-ism considerably stronger than in any previous period of English history when a domestic government was in office: under a foreign or a predominantly class government, such sympathy with Robin Hood-like figures was present, but it very seldom extended so widely among classes who had something to lose from public disorder. The individual can-not test the leadership qualities of his rulers, since the execu-tive protects them from comparisons—he treats them increasingly along the characteristic lines of thought which we find reserved for out-groups—in hostile or friendly stereo-types, as an alien 'they' upon whom the individual is depen-dent for elementary needs, but for whom he need entertain no moral respect.

Acquiescence in delinquent policies is in part a reflection of this sense of impotence. The individual is addressed as an individual, and in isolation, by the entire sales and enforce-ment organization. Unless he himself is overwhelmingly menaced by the proposed policy, and even when he is so menaced, he lacks the personal and cultural energy to differ. In wartime, part of this acquiescence is the acceptance of the official interpretation of the war: the citizen both agrees to acquiesce, and agrees to blame the public enemy for what has occurred. Once this has taken place, often after a parti-cular event which fixes the projection against the enemy, the stimulus-effect of war becomes apparent—the group-feeling of the nation, the sense of purpose and leadership, the release of crisis-anxiety in actual war, all tend to make rejection of the commitment more and more difficult.* It

* Most men . . . came to accept military life with reservations. Others found adjustment impossible, and, in spite of preinduction psychiatric examination, demonstrated traits of maladjustment necessitating their re-lease, or, if they revolted too belligerently, commitment to a penal institu-tion or mental hospital.'—G. L. Fahey and M. M. Mintz (1946), op. cit.

may persist through hardship and even despite certain defeat: the acquiescence once secured gains force with the progress of events. How far it can be presumed upon by the legislators will depend on the extent to which the war situation has been created before actual hostilities begin: Nazi Germany secured it by the entire repertoire of political tyranny, to the point at which even tacit disapproval of delinquent actions was minimal, before the outbreak of the second World War. In Britain, the public which accepted the atomic bomb in 1946 would have been less likely to accept it in 1940, and would have withheld its support from any form of indiscriminate warfare in 1936 by a large majority.

4: 2 The Corps d'Élite

A *corps d'élite* implies a body with special skills and, as a rule, special traditions, selected and raised for a purpose. In the past, the name and the function have been predominantly military. The military *élite*, viewed historically, shades off into hereditary military and ruling castes on one hand, into the technological groups—research teams, craftsmen— and into the semi-autonomous Commando units of modern war. Military *élite* troops, domestic or mercenary, have a long historical association with enforcement and security. The domestic enforcement-*élite*, while it existed on a semi-military basis in Sparta, Imperial Rome, and other societies, is a relatively recent development in Western Europe, which began to take shape in the nineteenth century.

Military *élite* units have shown two main lines of tradition —a tradition of prowess and performance, and a tradition of obedience. Some, such as the crews of small naval vessels operating independently, or the Chindits, have developed in recent years into patterns indistinguishable from 'comradeship' groups, and have tended to behave like small *ad hoc* primitive societies: the tradition of the enforcement-*élite* however, is generally, by the nature of its activities, concentrated in unquestioning obedience. The main cohering force of these bodies is, under modern conditions, a common repudiation of responsibility for the orders which they carry out.

The existence of this type of organization, and of this attitude of transferred responsibility, is particularly important in the mechanism of group delinquency. We have seen that while delinquent policies commonly originate among the legislative group, they generally do so at the fantasy level. In the consideration of ordinary personal delinquency, barriers between the wish and the deed appear at two points —when the individual seeks to rationalize his meditated action, and when he is confronted with the physical act which he meditates. There is, as we are all aware, a definite barrier between delinquent fantasy and delinquent performance. Most normal individuals might well meditate acts they would hesitate to commit, even while applauding them in others. The legislator is not called to put his own policies into physical effect—both in conception and in execution by others, their impact on his own experience is that of fantasy rather than action. The importance of the *élite* enforcement body is that it lies on the other side of this barrier. It can also justify actions which it regards with disfavour in terms of its tradition of loyal obedience.

Military groups have commonly reconciled their tradition of pride in performance with their tradition of loyalty by an exaggerated emphasis on their dependence upon orders: 'theirs not to reason why'. They may easily derive something very like satisfaction from the consequences of a blunder in the civilian administration. Even among troops in wartime, the physical effects of such mismanagement by 'brass hats' or civilians produce resentment more rapidly than they produce mutiny. The fantasy of war as a profession having no place for the estimation of goals or consequences, and of the soldier obeying orders he knows to be disastrous, and dying as the victim of his tradition of devotion, still has force in civilian armies.

The newer types of *élite*, the political police or the S.S., show a further exaggeration of this attitude. Delinquency outside the traditional pattern (the 'laws of war', 'soldierly conduct') was not likely to be acceptable to civilized armies of the older pattern, even when it was committed in deference to orders. The enforcement-*élite* has no comparable tradition. It has, however, an even more complete tradition of abrogated responsibility than its military counterpart. Its function is to carry out orders unquestioningly, in the same spirit as they were carried out by foreign bodyguard troops under the Roman Empire, without reference to the mores of the community and without respect of person. The givers of orders to such a body are a complete and externalized conscience. Where the *élite* force is highly politicized, this obedience may be a facet of general fanaticism. Even in this case, however, the behaviour of individual members tends to subsist at two different levels, one for daily use in personal affairs, derived from individual standards, and the other associated with the official capacity, where the tradition of duty is a complete answer to all criticism, from within or without. The policy-maker's assessment of the orders which he gives is blunted by the fact that he is separated from their physical execution—that of the executive by the fact that it is not responsible for them. The enforcement-*élite* lies on the far side of the barrier between intention and action. The politician is spared the pain of his decision, the executive the responsibility. Between the two, both the normal barriers which interpose between motive and act are by-passed or overstepped.

Even in societies which do not rely on the direct coercion of their home public, by political police or by troops, centralization has led to an increase in the number of irresponsible or potentially irresponsible *élite* groups. Even innocuous proposals which are readily defended on other grounds, such as the training by the Government of its own research staff in atomic physics from adolescent apprenticeship, are potential sources of such groups. Medical science and psychiatry might very easily incur similar risks. The total number of human beings who have adopted institutional abrogation of responsibility in one form or another has undoubtedly increased in the last twenty years, and this process is probably a more important factor in the growth of totalitarianism than purely economic or administrative 'control'. Where these *élites* contain potential delinquents, and especially where they attract or select them, delinquent fantasies and attitudes may very easily 'feed back' from the higher executive into the legislature, the authors thereby ridding themselves of responsibility for putting them into effect.

Psychoanalytical study of enforcement-*élites* is not yet very fully developed.* Considerable work has been done, often at the instance of the State, upon military morale and psychology. The recruiting of a civilian into the army is probably similar in effect to the migration of a civilian into one of the enforcement-machines. It involves the growth of a familiar psychiatric pattern, the 'projection' into immediate and more remote superiors of the standard-setting power of the father, which, in the independent individual, is 'introjected'—in other words, the conscience is externalized. The process may greatly lighten the load which some individuals have to bear—others, whose introjection is more complete and whose use of their standards is more subject to conscious criticism, are apt to develop feelings of guilt. Since those who dislike delegating their freedom of judgment to others appear, in our own society at least, to break down or to lose 'operational efficiency' most readily, military psychiatry may well find itself asked to restore the projection and still the questioning of reason. War crimes trials have thrown a rather doubtful light on the issue of responsibility for orders. In the machinery of government and law, the assessment of this responsibility is rather more cynical than that expressed by the War Crime Courts. Few governments would dissent

* By far the best description of such an enforcement-machine in action, from the viewpoint of dynamic psychology, is that of E. Lingens-Reiner, *Prisoners of Fear*, Gollancz, 1949, dealing with the mentality and behaviour of concentration-camp guards and 'trusties' as seen by a prisoner.

62

from the view of the Judge Advocate at the Belsen trial (expressed in an entirely different context, when he congratulated the defending officers for their performance of an unpleasant duty) that the foundation of all discipline is an unquestioning obedience to orders. Few observers would have the courage to suggest that an officer who had attempted to prevent the use of the atom bomb by warning the enemy that it was coming would have been able to plead the type of human responsibility which Kraemer was expected to exhibit. The immediate task of those who create an irresponsible *élite* is the stabilizing of the individual's acceptance of his external conscience, and the direction of his aggressive and resentful impulses against the enemy (the 'evil father-figure'). If this system breaks down, the paternal, guiding, protective, and propelling force of authority may become the object of these resentments. Such a change, while it is the first step towards a rational movement to displace or resist delinquent government, is predictably uncongenial to those who depend upon the executive to carry out their plans and fantasies.*

4: 3 *Attitude of Social Psychiatry*

Centralized societies, then, have removed at least one of the most important bars to delinquent action by legislators and their executive, in the creation of a legislature which can enact its fantasies without witnessing their effects, and an executive which abdicates all responsibility for what it does in response to superior orders. The main residual bar to large-scale delinquency is the survival of individual standards, which are increasingly vulnerable to propaganda, and to the impact of a society which has little opportunity for sociality. We have here the counterpart of the change which has taken place in leadership and selection, and the harmful effects of both processes are additive. While these risks are real, we have to set against them the extreme vulnerability

* See E. Simmel in S. Lorand, *Psychoanalysis Today*, Allen & Unwin, 1949.

of the entire social apparatus upon which they depend to individual resistance and communal loss of morale. The strength of the enforcement machinery is largely a façade, which impresses the individual chiefly because he faces it alone, and political observers in social democracies uniformly over-estimate the power of the State to withstand shifts in public opinion. In approaching social delinquency, therefore, psychiatry need have no fear that it is challenging an inevitable historical process.

In any psychological study of society to-day, the irrational and the destructive emphases may well appear to predominate. There is, however, the abundant evidence of the dynamism and persistence of sociality, of individual impulses towards co-operation, integration, and social health. Irrational institutions are secure only so long as they can satisfy or divert the constructive side of their public's thought and attitude; once the irrationalities are felt, even if they are not consciously understood, as threats to home security, personal liberty, or individual life, the fabric of institutions is at once threatened. So long as the protest takes explicitly political forms, within the mechanism of social democracy, its power of effecting real change is limited by the factors which we have discussed. Once it manifests itself as public resentment, disillusion, or loss of obedience, sufficiently strong and sufficiently resistant to propaganda, the mechanism of enforcement, which is designed to coerce active individuals rather than passive majorities, is largely disarmed. It seems unlikely that any government which exists at the present time could surmount such a nation-wide loss of confidence. So far as the purely destructive aspects of revolution are concerned, the idol which, by conscription or exhortation, can repress the opposition or quiet the doubts of a public for whom its deity is not yet suspect, has feet of clay, once its power and its significance are challenged by attitudes rather than by parties. The degree of social delinquency which is possible in any society, our own included, is a function of the degree of acquiescence which the delinquents can command in their public. Beside the general public temper, the attitude of specific groups may prove a decisive barrier to an irrational policy. Scientific and technical workers occupy a vital position in the modern society, as do groups of public utility workers in transport production and mining. The conception of the General Strike, which played a large part in early socialist thought, was sociologically sound. Its political efficacy has been reduced more by the growth of Trade Unionism into a centralized pattern similar and allied to that of the State, than by any inherent power of governments to deal effectively with public refusal. As modern states have attempted to reinforce their police and military forces by selection and indoctrination, they have also attempted to extend similar guarantees of loyalty to other groups. This process is particularly obvious in connection with military science. A major safeguard against delinquent national policies is endangered whenever scientific workers consent to delegate their judgment or co-operate with authority under conditions which lie outside their own control.

Sociology and psychiatry, since they deal specifically with human society and attitude, are under a particularly strong obligation to scrutinize the conditions under which they cooperate with established authority. It might well be held that advances in the pattern of society depend upon the personal responsibility of practitioners in these studies more fully than upon that of any other group. Should social sciences become a new weapon of enforcement, the opportunity of the present age may well have been lost for an indefinite period.

II
THE STATE
AND HUMAN BEHAVIOR

'No laws are binding on the subject that assault
the person or violate the conscience.'

BLACKSTONE

1. FUNCTIONS OF THE STATE

1: 1 *Conceptions of Government*

WE have grown up with the State. It has existed in all civilized Western societies of which we have knowledge, and attempts to discover the first point at which government appeared in human society take us beyond the historical record and into a field of inference and guesswork. In fact, a search for such a beginning begs a question which we are in no position to answer: primitive societies which exist with the minimum of government often appear to represent a high stage of development and a response to local conditions, rather than a stage in the evolution of more complicated societies. We do not yet know enough of the society which exists among primates* to be able to draw conclusions from their behaviour, and it is doubtful how far observations on lower animals would help us to understand the more complex behaviour of men.

Each period of history has held characteristic ideas of the function of the state. In fact, these theories and their consequences are the basis of our historical classification. The institution preceded the attempts to justify it—many of these theories are the rationalizations of men who recognized its usefulness or saw no way of dispensing with its defects. The state preceded them, but has been profoundly altered by opinion. In our own century it has undertaken a vast new field of organizational and planning activity, and theory has expanded to take in the charge.

* See S. Zuckerman, *The Social Life of Monkeys and Apes* (Kegan Paul, 1932); G. H. Seward, *Sex and the Social Order* (McGraw Hill, 1946).

Most philosophers of the state have begun their argument from a hypothetical 'state of nature', on which government has been imposed with the growth of civilization. The philosophy of the state preceded the Christian tradition, but since the influence of the Greek philosophers was long submerged, and reappeared in the Renaissance to mould modern liberal democracy, political thought has undergone a series of fluctuations based on its estimate of man. What the democratic tradition has in common is its belief that the state is a mechanism whereby human conduct can be modified. The shifts in political thought are all shifts in our assumptions about the nature and impulses of individuals. For Hobbes, cultures without authority are unthinkable, for authority is the only guarantee of security. For Locke, man is social, and possesses an instinctive biological ethic, that 'no one ought to harm another in his life, health, liberty or possessions': there are those in whom this pattern is defective, and the state is the union of the sociable majority to repress them. 'Thus in the state of Nature, one man comes by a power over another . . . but only to retribute . . . so far as calm reason and conscience dictate what is proportionate to the transgression.'* For Rousseau, an intense personal hatred of coercion and a profound conviction of the innate goodness of man were not grounds for rejecting the state, so much as for distributing it piecemeal as widely as possible—if men tend to be innately good, and have been betrayed by those whom, in their generous innocence, they appointed to represent them, then the wider the participation in government, the greater the protection of the community against abnormal and aggressive individuals—'Whoso refuses to obey the general will shall be compelled to do so by the whole body'.†

These three philosophers have all been widely quoted in our own time, though not all by the same people. Hobbes, wrestling with the perennial problem of how to use force for the preservation of

* Locke, *Second Treatise of Government*, cited by Ranyard West, *Conscience and Society*, 1942.
† Rousseau, *Social Contract*, p. 18.

peace instead of for the perpetuation of war, tends to be quoted by the practical politician faced to-day with the same problem on the largest scale which this world can provide. Locke . . . is favoured by the lawyers; while Rousseau's flaming passion and metaphysical abstractions have made his resounding epigrams and paradoxes the inspiration at once of the social idealist and of a philosophical school which has taken the same title.*

Widely different was the view of Catholic orthodoxy that man, having rejected the government of God, must needs be subject to the government of man, if only to keep society together while the major drama of human life, its religious exercise, was carried out. For them, the state as a means of altering human conduct, except by the crudest coercion, gives place to the influence of the Church—the two may co-operate, but the civil authority is no more than the Church's bodyguard. Laws and institutions cannot regenerate those who are suffering from spiritual diseases. For Milton, in another Christian tradition, the state is appointed by the individual as a means of ensuring *his own* good conduct, as Dr. Johnson, in fear of insanity, kept handcuffs in his house so that his friends might prevent him from doing mischief.

All these theories, with their elements of truth, have modified attitudes to the state and forms of government without radically altering the type of activity which the state in fact undertakes. In looking at their authors' life histories we can trace the sources of their emphases and conjectures, but their views of man were, at root, conjectural views. They had only limited knowledge of societies outside their own tradition, they shared a considerable moral agreement which belonged to the intellectual custom of Europe, and they adopted a superficial view of human motives. That individuals could actively desire pain, punishment, or unprofitable hardship was not a conception with which they were familiar.

At the present time we are dealing with newer philo-

* Ranyard West, op. cit.

71

sophies of the state, but most of these are, in analysis, expansions or combinations of the ideas canvassed by Hobbes, Locke and Rousseau, or by their predecessors and their successors. Neither Marxism nor Fascism contribute anything fundamentally new to the controversy, however much they emphasize change in the form and scope of the state. It is doubtful if there is anything new to add. The revolution in political thought comes not from any fresh perception of the issues, but from the fact that it is becoming possible to verify the various conjectures which older thinkers made in their treatment of man. No universal agreement is yet in sight between psychologists over the factual material, but the whole subject has already passed out of the field of mere opinion into the field of experimental research.

The public emphasis has also changed. Earlier opinion looked primarily to law and government to protect their persons and property from individual criminals, private or public. Modern opinion shows a growing concern with the protection of individuals against the activities of states. The individual to-day is far less menaced by local gangsterism than by the aggression, tyranny, or suppression of rights which he anticipates from the governments of other countries, or of his own. British public opinion has a long-standing *modus vivendi* with authority, which it regards without either malice or enthusiasm, and we find it difficult to put ourselves in the shoes of less secure and more frequently invaded or dominated countries. Denunciations of the state in England are generally denunciations of a particular party by its opponents, and carry the assumption that provided the denouncers are in office, the state is a beneficial institution. In spite of this reasonable, or complacent, approach, it is difficult in the light of modern knowledge to look at the processes of democratic government with as much optimism as our fathers did. Since we began to study the state as a part of society, rather than a theoretical function, we have not been able to exclude considerations of public health, mental as well as physical—institutional government to-day is part

72

of a pattern of centralization in all fields of life, and there is no possible ground for complacency over the total effect of this pattern. The kind of progress envisaged by the earlier liberal depended on such factors as an informed electorate, an absence of gross social and mental disorders, and a predominance of reason over prejudice. There is considerable ground for doubt whether centralized urban orders can meet these conditions at a purely biological and physical level. Even the powers of orthodox law to repress crime are severely tested by a society which has managed to undermine the older mores without providing anything to replace them.

At the same time, our questioning of the assumptions which were formerly made about the function of the state has been carried further. For the earlier theorists, men were greedy or violent by nature or through moral depravity. Our ideas of human nature have become a good deal less rigid. We know that in most cases of antisocial behaviour, trains of intelligible causation can be made out. The more these trains of causation become obvious, the stronger is the need to re-examine the activities of the state in the light of its supposed functions—to what extent are modern states in fact conducive to social behaviour? To what extent do laws in fact serve to modify human conduct? The simple estimate of government as the expression of a general will towards moral order has been materially shaken by a series of acts of delinquency committed not by individuals but by ostensibly civilized states. The clear-cut line dividing the moral will of the community from the outlawed activities of criminals cannot stand up to the scrutiny of modern psychiatry—we have too much evidence of similarity between the processes of moral and of immoral behaviour, and of the tendency to rationalize our conduct, for any simple estimate to be possible.

I: 2 *Coercion as a Socializing Force*

Part of our political tradition is the belief that if any type of conduct proves undesirable, it can be removed, or at least effectively prevented, by legal prohibition. The reason that we have fewer murders than, for instance, Corsica, or less prostitution than France or Japan, lies in the fact that we have better laws. There is surprisingly little evidence to support this view. In the first place, history is full of unsuccessful attempts to repress particular forms of conduct by law. Granted a sufficient incentive, and an absence of public condemnation of the prohibited action, severity of penalty has little to do with the outcome of such attempts. Laws which run counter to accepted public standards, or which prohibit actions which the public regards neutrally, are hardly ever enforceable. The law is, it seems, only effective in supplementing the mores of the community in which it exists, not in forming them. Kinsey *et al.** have stated that under existing American law one male citizen in three could be imprisoned for his sexual conduct, if every violation were to be detected and prosecuted. Vigorous laws only repress crime if they can do it by suppressing criminals—the suppression of gangsterism in the United States was possible largely because the social conditions which produced the supply of gangsters did not recur in the same form. It is extremely difficult to estimate how far fear of punishment prevents individuals from committing crime—in many cases it seems rather to modify the form of antisocial activity which is chosen. In the second place, the growth of the authority and effectiveness of the state in centralized orders has been outpaced by the growth of individual crime. With the removal of public scrutiny and local mores which accompanied the growth of industrial city communities, the number of individuals whose social conscience is strong enough to be effectively supplemented by law has almost certainly decreased. At the same time, an enormous growth of administrative law has produced innumerable offences which have no basis in everyday standards. The public stigma of prosecution is reduced. In these large communities it is very

* Kinsey, Pomeroy & Martin, *Sexual behaviour of the human male,* 1948.

doubtful whether changes in institutions can ever effectively alter the pattern of events—history and conduct are so much influenced by biological and social forces that their progress is increasingly out of control, so far as the legislators are concerned. Older laws to some extent crystallized the general public will—modern laws are less able to do so, since the public will is less definite, and the opportunities for expressing it socially are curtailed. For the first time in history laws are effectively 'made' by the state, without evoking any very marked response in the internal standards of the individual.

When we consider delinquent actions by the state itself, the 'war crimes' with which we are familiar, the liberal tradition turns naturally to a reapplication of the method which it upheld in local affairs—governments must be placed under the control and coercion of a World government, which can prevent misconduct as the local state prevents crime. This attempt to carry the pattern of centralization a stage further inspires no confidence whatever in the light of our study of the mechanisms which determine individual conduct. The greater the degree of power, and the wider the gap between governors and governed, the stronger the appeal of office to those who are likely to abuse it, and the less the response which can be expected from the individual. Super-governments have succeeded, as the Roman Church succeeded for a while, when they could appeal directly to the mores of the public. Public social sense which transcends frontiers is a fact, and it persists, but it has so far failed to restrain local governments from aggressive actions. Who is to repress the world authority when it 'too' falls into the wrong hands?

We have to recognize that the psychopathic government is an outgrowth to-day of the centralized and increasingly psychopathic public. It is also the most important vested interest in the continuance of centralization. If individual conduct is to be regulated primarily by laws and institutions, the centralized order is overwhelmingly superior to less unified patterns. The failure of the state to wither away is implicit in its assumptions. The organizational aspect of its work becomes continually more deeply confused with the repressive and the regulative. The growth of an asocial public, dependent on central direction for the standards it lacks, ensures that the time will never be ripe for any return of function to the public at large. The temptation is to hang on a little longer, to centralize further, if only to save the immediate situation. Even where the discoveries of sociology make contact with the legislature, their implementation is something to be put off until 'after the final victory' or 'after the end of the emergency'. Cultures which gravitate into a chronic emergency can postpone them indefinitely. The time for the revolution is never ripe.

2. POWER AND THE 'NATURAL' MAN

2:1 *Normality*

IN deciding the 'normality' or otherwise of the desire for power, we run the risk of becoming involved in an argument similar to that about the 'state of nature'—normality readily comes to imply the pattern of conduct which meets with the psychiatrist's approval. Where a similar argument exists over the 'normality' of various forms of sexual behaviour, it rapidly becomes obvious that statistical averages are not comments on the desirability of a given pattern of conduct. If by normality we mean the same thing as the physician understands by the word 'health', we have to give it some significance of optimal function. The meaning of 'optimal' in turn depends on our standards. The statistically normal citizen of contemporary cultures suffers from an anxiety state which is in no sense 'optimal'. In discussing the abuse of power, we have certain standards implicit in the discussion —'normality' is the status of the society, seen in its individual member, which encounters the fewest destructive stresses, which functions most satisfactorily to its members. This kind of utilitarianism is based on a rather longer view than that of the greatest immediate good to the greatest number: it takes into consideration the realization of human potentialities as a whole, the growth of human control over the universe, and over human affairs. In begging these questions we need to be clear in our minds exactly what questions are being begged. We can to some extent answer the dispute over the 'natural' state of man by pointing to societies which seem to function with a minimum of friction

77

and surplus aggression, as well as to the highly 'unnatural' type of health and immunity from epidemic disease which exists in scientific cultures.

The best picture which we can secure of the human condition, as seen by science, goes back in essence to Hobbes. Human life, which, in the face of the physical universe, is unquestionably 'solitary, poor, nasty, brutish and short' evokes human powers of adjustment to render it sociable, comfortable, secure, cultured, and long. Man applies his intelligence to secure an equilibrium with his environment not by abandoning his values but by modifying the environment. This application gives all science, including psychiatry and social medicine, its terms of reference. Unlike earlier religious cultures, we are in a position to make life itself and humanity the primary standards of reference. If it is argued that human mortality and the magnitude-scale of the universe make human aspirations to security and achievement unrealizable, we can only reply that the normal expectation of life does not significantly affect our use of the term 'health' in medicine as a goal to be pursued, if not reached, and that it is not yet possible to class any physical achievement as permanently outside the reach of science.

2: 2 Sociology of Power

It is not here possible to deal at all fully with the comparative sociology of power.

The appearance of organized government in primitive societies has been related to the rise of hunting as a group activity, and to the appearance of private property. It is almost certainly related to the development of organized war. A more interesting observation is the parallel appearance of organized government and of antisocial patterns of behaviour.* This can be interpreted in two ways—if the state is the community's attempt to safeguard itself against social disorder and disintegration, its rise can be regarded as

* W. F. Ogburn and M. F. Nimkoff, *A Handbook of Sociology* (Kegan Paul, London, 1947). See also R. H. Lowie, *Origin of the State*.

a response to new stresses, and to the breakdown of older and simpler forms of individual adjustment. It is also possible, however, that the stress factors which produced the supply of delinquents provided the supply of power-seekers.

Unfortunately, no definite information is available on the relative numbers of abnormals in primitive and modern society. The percentage may have been smaller among peoples who lived in the hunting culture, for it was a type of society in which human beings had lived for hundreds of thousands of years, and hence had probably worked out a fairly satisfactory adjustment. . . . Those abnormals who remain may not be regarded as problems or menaces. It should be noted that the religions of many primitive groups are such as to socialize the conduct of those who seem to have neurotic tendencies.*

No close parallel can yet be drawn between the picture of the rise of government which we derive from social anthropology, and that of the origins of the desire for power which we derive from psychoanalysis. It seems likely that at the point in any culture when it ceases to be capable of absorbing its own abnormal members, the demand for coercion appears hand in hand with the emergence of individuals who desire to coerce.

There is a good deal of evidence that in cultures where the main task resembles that of science, to maintain life and society in the face of external difficulties, competition for power accounts for an extremely small part of the total energy of individuals. Cohesion of this kind in the face of an external threat occurs in our own society. The desire for approval and love is also demonstrably a fundamental part of the make-up of individuals. It plays a large part in determining deliberate attempts to secure status. The limits which determine its expression are based on the self-appointed task of the culture concerned, as embodied in its standards. The warrior is a figure of admiration to warlike tribes, and the proficient thief to communities of thieves. On an entirely superficial assessment of motives, many forms of delinquency are roundabout means of securing the type of

* W. F. Ogburn and M. F. Nimkoff, Op. cit.

approval which the individual desires; where society, or the individual's own attitude, deny it, money may buy, or position enforce it. The psychoanalytical explanation of society begins by drawing attention to the fact that it is in the approval or disapproval of our parents that we first experience this basic desire. Freud's main contribution to the theory of society was in showing the interaction between this desire and the equally fundamental sexual development of the individual. Throughout life the two are parallel, and the distinction is even less clear cut in childhood, when sexuality is not tied to the specific pattern of adult reproductive behaviour. In most human societies, as in some higher animals, the father tends to occupy a special position as the source of parental approval, the administrator of rewards and punishments, and an alternate source of pleasure and frustration. He is alternately admired as a model of strength, wisdom and success, and resented as an object of jealousy and a barrier to the child's sexual and non-sexual ambitions. So far as we can guess, the earliest form of social hierarchy may well have been a family of families based on the dynamic position of fatherhood.

The striking differences between 'power-centred' and 'life-centred' cultures are closely analogous to the differences between power-seeking and life-seeking individuals. Almost all the existing evidence suggests that the psychoanalytical view of such differences, which attributes them to identification with one or other parent, has widespread value in interpreting cultural as well as individual behaviour. In the most typical instances, the 'patriform' society, based upon jealousy of the father, concentrates its prohibitions upon sex and disobedience to authority, the 'matriform' against offences which threaten the food supply.* Both civilized and primi-

* The detailed work of Mead (M. Mead, *Co-operation and Competition Among Primitive Peoples*, McGraw Hill, New York, 1937), makes it clear that a far more complicated classification of primitive society-types is possible, but the distinction between power-centred and life-centred cultures and cultural elements is identifiable in almost all primitive societies.

tive societies are fairly easily divisible between these two types—among modern political groups classical 'patriform' societies occasionally appear, in which death or castration are typical punishments, and the status of women is lowered. Nazi Germany was one such example. With the growth of centralization, however, it is possibly more accurate to describe modern societies as effecting a division between 'patriform' individuals, who gravitate into government and enforcement, and 'matriform' individuals who enter fields where co-operation, production, and creation are more important than command, prohibition and coercion.* There is, it seems, a good deal of evidence, both from sociology and individual psychiatry, for the view that modern government may select a particular and a maladjusted section of the community when it recruits its members.

How much sexual content we find in these infantile attitudes will depend to some extent on our definition of sexuality. The attempt to express all dynamic psychology in terms of the Oedipus situation is probably an over-simplification, and leaves us with the need to explain why the existence of incestuous impulses is so strongly repudiated by the child. It is, however, demonstrably true that social standards are derived directly from parental example, and that the 'conscience' is formed, in content at least, by these standards coupled to the desire to win approval. Independent social sense does not emerge fully until early adolescence, by which time the child's attitude towards its fellows is already largely fixed in terms of its attitude towards the father. The desire for power appears to be, in many cases, an attempt to establish the kind of status which the father held, and which the child admired or envied. The desire to obey is almost an equal component of the political pattern, and this in turn can be regarded as a carry-over into adult life of a yearning for the security of the nursery with its external standards.

Aggression, another component of adult delinquency, is by no means an abnormal or necessarily an undesirable ele-

*See J. C. Flügel, *Man, Morals and Society*, 1945.

ment. Humanity maintains itself by an aggressive attitude toward its environment—interpersonal aggression is at root a desire to recognize and to be recognized; to avoid being ignored or isolated. To this extent at least 'hate is the precursor of love'. Sadism in its Freudian sense is almost certainly a primary mammalian impulse, in which elements of aggression, the seeking for dynamic relationships, and a desire for pursuit and capture or for strong skin stimulation during mating combine. The type of sadism which features in the discussion of political and military atrocities is an outgrowth of this: the desire to inflict suffering as a means to, or a substitute for, normal sexual and socio-sexual relationships.

Freud regarded sadism, in its more general sense, as a primary impulse which is converted into masochism, the desire to suffer or to submit, only where it provokes a reaction of guilt in the subject. West (op. cit.) in his study of aggression in society points to some of the difficulties of this view: a desire to suffer is probably more fundamental to the individual than Freud himself suspected. Freud certainly recognized the 'willingness to suffer pain on the circuitous route to pleasure' which contributes to many of the more complicated patterns of conduct that confound simple theories of human social history as a pursuit of happiness.

From all this we can identify the components of the desire for power as:

(1) simple patterns of dominance;

(2) self-identification with the coercive father, and a desire to imitate his status;

(3) power as a sexual substitute, or as a form of compensation for failure to secure status and affection elsewhere;

(4) the attitude of societies which offer political power as a legitimate and approved activity.

These carry their own converse in the desire for obedience:

(1) as an acceptance of the dominance of others;

(2) as a perpetuation of childhood behaviour, and the desire for security of status through submission;

(3) as a means of reconciling sadism with the disapproval and resistance which it evokes;

(4) as a positive duty, inculcated by tradition.

Any attempt to apply rigid ideas of 'normality' to these patterns runs into immediate difficulties, whether the normal implies prevalence or desirability. Dominance patterns are apparently inseparable from all types of relationship among men and animals, and political authority only accounts for some of them. Identification with the father is also in essence a normal pattern—moral deficiency in various forms seems to be associated with an absence of home security, and it looks as if abnormal and harmful emphases only occur when the element of coercion and force in the father-image is unduly prominent: the identification in this case may take the form of rebellion or of an overmastering desire to inflict on others the type of authority which the father imposes. To this extent coercive 'patriform' societies perpetuate their structure through coercive family relationships. The association of power and pain-inflicting behaviour with sexuality is undoubtedly a neurosis in its social manifestations, if we define a neurosis as the fixed repetition of inappropriate behaviour in response to conflict, and it is one which the withholding of sexual outlets in our own society appears to propagate. The emphasis in centralized society which plays the most important part in producing militant political tyrannies is probably the desire for a continuance of the external, parental, conscience into adult life. The strain of dependence on individual judgment, and the lack of status which the adult feels in centralized, asocial life are prominent causes of the unlimited and masochistic obedience which Fascism demands, and democracy may occasionally obtain.* Obedience in modern societies is more often a hideous vice than a Christian virtue.

What is striking about these elements in social behaviour is that the better the individual adjustment, the more easily they are absorbed in ordinary patterns of living, and the less

* See E. Fromm, *The Fear of Freedom*, 1940.

incentive remains to make them a basis for an overmastering impulse to regulate the behaviour of others. The closest connection between power and abnormality is in the essentially uncreative and unproductive nature of the impulse to regulate by prohibition. This impulse is almost always the expression of a failing, rather than a successful, adaptation. We try to prohibit those things which inspire guilty, resentful, or jealous feelings: prohibition is a substitute for participation. The prohibition of indecency is a standby of those for whom sexual experience is a source of guilt and distaste: the prohibition of wealth may represent the reaction of the man who has been deprived of its benefits and insulted by its possessors. To some extent the prohibition of delinquency is the reaction of those who have a deep-rooted community of desire with the delinquent. Like Dr. Johnson, they are forging their own handcuffs.

The modern conception of 'human nature' in psychiatry, in so far as it is united and articulate, has been well stated by Fleming.

The problem of the educator is not so much that of 'training' towards spontaneous kindliness, initiative, honesty or emotional sincerity as of permitting opportunities for these attributes to reveal themselves. The child, the adolescent or the adult is not merely a 'savage' or a 'beast' whose anti-social impulses towards self-assertion, cruelty, or greed require to be restrained; but a human being —social in nature ('a son of God')—who is capable of evil as well as good but who can find satisfaction only in the 'good'. In an atmosphere of frustration, aggression, discouragement and neglect he will appear aggressive, cruel, anti-social and inhibited; but removal of such influences will result in the revelation of a new creature.

Abundant evidence on these lines has been collected in the last twenty years from experiments in the situational treatment of problem children, and (more recently) from observation of the re-education of Nazified youth and the rehabilitation of neurotic prisoners of war. Human beings are social. They need to give affection, to exercise responsibility, and to attain insight; and in the absence of imposed frustrations and the presence of the complementary affection, trust and patient encouragement of friendly and receptive groups, they have been observed to blossom into social virtues whose flowering appeared impossible under other sorts of husbandry.*

The violence of the contrast between this view and the idea of government as a weight placed upon the lid of human delinquent impulses to keep it down is not softened by the close connection between the administrative encouragement of large centralized aggregates and the denial of precisely those conditions of social and personal development which this modern body of experience advocates. Centralized society fails to provide these conditions either for the rulers or the ruled, and the reactions of both combine to threaten its violent collapse. Politics against this background is seen less as a delinquent activity of power-drunk individuals— the stereotype which appeals to the revolutionary when he is out of office—than as an activity which is unprofitable in itself, since its presuppositions contradict its purposes. Almost all its remedies aggravate the type of behaviour they profess to eliminate. The addictive elements in political office, which Acton recognized, might well make scientific sociology unwilling to give more than a guarded support to measures of decentralization which involve the election of individuals to office. It prefers to deal directly with the individual, through education and the setting up of experimental communities which fulfil the requirements laid down by scientific study.

* Fleming, *Adolescence*. p. 210, 1948, Routledge and Kegan Paul.

3. REMEDIES

3: 1 *Revolution*

THIS is an age of discouraged revolutionaries. The nineteenth-century pattern of violent social change from below commands the full allegiance of serious sociologists only in those countries which lagged behind in the pattern of centralization—the Balkan States, Spain and Italy, the Communist States and the emergent nationalist movements of the East. Revolution in its original liberal and radical significance is revolution towards, rather than against, centralization. It takes over all the assumptions concerning the function of the state which exist in the parliamentary tradition—its object is, in fact, the capture of institutions to redress grievances.

Part of the discomfiture of English revolutionary bodies of all complexions comes from the appreciation that the nineteenth-century notion of a *levée-en-masse* against class oppressors had little reality: revolutions which have succeeded have invariably been organized around a rival government, a closely knit directing body which has depended upon popular feeling for its support, but which has been concerned primarily to take over the existing legislative and enforcement mechanism. Another unfavourable factor is that the inevitable progress of urban population towards discontented insurrection, foreseen by the early socialists, has been decisively halted in some societies by the palliation of the worst features of industrialism and a distinct increase in material comfort. The centralized society no longer invariably provides a militantly revolutionary proletariat. The

86

chief threat to this superficial stability comes from the boom-to-slump oscillation of centralized economies, but the manifestations of discontent, when they do appear, are directed by the whole pattern of urban social life into channels which lead towards aggravations of the centralized pattern. If social-democratic governments are violently overthrown under these conditions, it is by more extreme forms of hierarchy based on exaggerations of their own irrational attitudes —Fascism, Nazi-ism, or totalitarian Communism. Revolution under these conditions is generally a final stabilization of the pattern of the permanent war economy as a solution to outstanding difficulties. Like war, it gains its support by creating a sense of civic purpose, and directing attention to stereotype enemies. The first task of any revolutionary administration is to ensure that the change of control does not seriously derange the detailed working of the community—the second is to provide itself with an enforcement executive capable of interposing between itself and the public at large.

Of the revolutionary movements in Europe, only the Anarchists differ from the preconceived ideas of state function which existing governments uphold. The earliest theorists of anarchism, such as William Godwin and Kropotkin, strikingly anticipate the findings of sociology in their estimate of human behaviour and the means of modifying conduct. The quaintness of Godwin's suggestion that a free individual should not deign to play in an orchestra under a conductor is less obvious if we state it in terms of the restriction of art to professionals which is one of many types of vicarious living in modern society. Godwin did not forsee the wide availability of this type of centralized art which technology has provided, and might not have accepted its value if he had. Kropotkin profoundly influenced human biology by his theory of mutual aid, propounded as a counterblast to the social conclusions drawn from the Darwinian 'struggle for existence'. He was one of the first systematic students of animal communities, and may be regarded as the founder of modern social ecology. The actual and visible tendency towards central organization as a requisite for technological progress weighted the balance heavily against the anarchist wing of the radical movement. As a potential mass movement, anarchism retains its strength only in Spain, where an anarchist community was set up during the Civil War, and in Italy. It retains its nineteenth-century ideology only in cultures where industrialism did not fully disrupt the pattern of rural communal life, and where the idea of local self-sufficiency has never appeared chimerical or retrogressive.

The forces which mould the individual revolutionary are at least as complex as those which mould governments. Psychopaths of the power-acquisitive type, schizophrenics, and theorists taking refuge in utopian schemes may all participate: some at least are people who, in a different context, would become institutional rulers. Flügel* has summarized the role of reactions to parental authority in the production of rebels of this type.

It is, however, as groundless to identify all revolutionary thought with psychopathy as it is to detect signs of insanity in all institutional rulers. Whatever irrational attitudes emerge in the course of revolutions are evoked by real defects in society. The psychiatry which identifies all discontent with society as a manifestation of ill-health, calling for 'readjustment', denies its own vocation. Suggestions that the working classes strike more often than the professional because of the more brutal parental discipline in their homes† or that 'agitators, conscientious objectors, fanatics, publicists and cranks'‡ fall automatically in the class of anti-social unmodifiable psychopaths, exhibit an insensitivity to realities which psychiatry can ill afford. We can allow at least as much recognition of the part of unconscious processes in the psychology of social agitation as in the psychology of govern-

* J. C. Flügel, *The Psychoanalytic Study of the Family*, 1938.
† C. Burt, cited by Flügel, op. cit.
‡ H. S. Hulbert, cited by Norwood East, op. cit.

ment without losing sight of the fact that the merit of adaptation depends on the circumstances to which the patient is being asked to adapt. The redirection of aggressive impulses produced by asocial living against the pattern of asociality, rather than against external stereotypes, is no more than the counterpart of the mechanism by which humanity has overcome smallpox and cholera, and is an eminently acceptable outlet for such impulses, provided that it takes the form of rational and fully conscious disobedience by intelligent individuals towards irresponsible institutions. That the material of such a revolution exists is evident from clinical practice. Whenever the social psychologist points out to the individual the reasons for his inability to find satisfaction in existing patterns of society, he is performing an obligatory and entirely necessary work of subversion.

We find the revolutionary obligations of psychiatry easier to accept in the context of Fascism or Communism than in our own system. Few if any psychotherapists would wish to 'readjust' the S.S. man or the *Totenkommando* leader to his occupation. Both science and the public of centralized order underestimate their own power to restrain group delinquency by individual action. It has been repeatedly suggested that the concentration of military power in the hands of the state renders effective resistance impossible. In terms of the actionist fantasy of nineteenth-century radicals, this is undoubtedly true, but the centralized war-state is probably more vulnerable to individual disobedience than any previous type of culture, by reason of its dependence upon technology and acquiescence. We have seen the precarious balance which such states maintain whenever they engage in war or in civil persecution. Defensive and offensive wars conducted by large states, by means of civilian armies, are wholly at the mercy of individual morale, and military powers devote immense energy to its maintenance. The threat of domination by external enemies has done much to obscure the fact that defensive war is itself a conscious governmental choice—the legislature which has to face a thoroughly unreliable public is likely to display a diplomatic caution similar to that of states which possess no reasonable chance of resisting aggression by arms. Under present conditions, where defensive as well as offensive war is incompatible with individual and national survival, such an attitude may be held to provide a valuable safeguard.

The bringing about of this state of affairs is, in fact, an almost inevitable consequence of the spread of modern sociology in social democracies, and the changes in warfare and in Britain's world status may well accelerate it. The toleration of war by the British public has diminished from conflict to conflict, and although we cannot over-estimate the durability of the change, or underestimate the efficacy of propaganda in arousing fear and acquiescence, the progress of a deep-seated change in attitude cannot always be gauged by the surface of opinion. An estimate of effective war-resistance in Britain to-day would have to include not only the vocal conscientious objectors, but the larger group of non-conscientious objectors who express themselves in desertion, skrimshanking, and possibly also in psychosomatic breakdown, whether they profess to accept war as an institution or not. However the necessities of war may be rationalized, the modern combatant public exhibits manifestations of guilt and disquiet which belie their conscious acquiescence.

It has been suggested that the growth of social sense may render nations unfit to withstand the attacks of their less-scrupulous neighbours.* The process, however, is not one which can be reversed. We cannot have it both ways. Either social psychology will devote itself to cultivating positive attitudes based on human responsibility, whatever the consequences, or it must cease to exist as an independent science and accept a purely veterinary status. Like the effects of atomic energy, we cannot select and reject certain consequences of knowledge—we can only accommodate ourselves to the whole pattern of our results. The irrelevance of

* M. Mead at the International Congress on Mental Health, 1948.

military victory in terms of total war, and the knowledge of the nature of the consequences of defence on economical and cultural life, provide added grounds for declining to abandon the struggle.

To a great extent, the idea of the indefensibility of social cultures is true only if we think in terms of military and institutional defences of the kind advocated by the state. Such cultures are highly resistant to outside interference, and this resistance is all the more effective because it is not dependent on organization. Centralized societies like our own have no cultural defence in depth; their defeat is always total. Once the crust of military protection is broken, the state has exhausted its resources, and may regard it as an obligation to hand over the executive to the victors in the interests of law and order. Predominantly social societies depend for their integrity on the patterns of life and belief of individuals and small groups. One of the essential weaknesses of asociality is that it has no adequate defences against tyrants, domestic or foreign—by inculcating patterns of life which may express themselves in independence and in resistance to central authority when this appears necessary, we are actually creating a public which is better able to look after itself than the society of conformists on which military defence depends. If resistance to outside aggression by these means involves the acceptance of loss, risk, suffering, and a partial retrogression of society, it may be held that such risks are not greater than those of successful defensive war at the present time. The features of national life—political sovereignty, institutions, the state itself, which military leaders aim to defend, are less significant in the value scale of civilization than sociality, stability, and individual judgment.

Responsible sociology must recognize, however, a sense of urgency in conducting its propaganda: the stage of transition, in which individuals are disgusted and distrustful towards the existing pattern, without having had time to form a stable new one, is particularly likely to produce catastrophes. In view of the mechanism by which attitudes are formed, the transition cannot occupy much less than a generation, and if we are to stabilize our culture in the modern world we should clearly devote more time to practical and educational work outside the existing pattern and based on first principles.

Whether revolution takes place suddenly or gradually is more a matter of circumstance and event than of choice. The historical 'revolution' is usually only the coming to a head of such a process of gradual attitude-change. Decisive action may be required, but not as an element in a revolution-fantasy. The transition from asocial to social living takes place at the level which religious apostles term 'life changing' rather than at the barricades, and any violence which it involves is more likely to come from the exponents of older pattern, who still regard institutional coercion as a means of 'saving the Republic', than from the revolutionaries themselves.

By far the most serious criticism of the orthodox and Marxist conception of revolution, as it is stated by critical and intelligent students of society, such as Caudwell,* arises from the extent of the change which such a revolution is expected to produce by mainly institutional methods. That revolutionary governments can infuse a new social integration into their publics is not in question: to this extent, revolution does modify and improve individual adjustment in cultures where lack of objective is a cause of ill-health. This, however, can occur without reference to the social objectives of the movement. Nazi-ism was largely successful in revivifying German group feeling. The methods of the revolutionaries are almost always, however, identical with those used by asocial ruling groups in wartime—projection, mobilization of group resentment against stereotypes, and a political or geographical nationalism of class or state.† Even

* C. Caudwell, *Illusion and Reality, Studies in a Dying Culture*, 1938.
† 'Widespread misery and depression do not of themselves cause revolutions. Before revolution can occur the misery of the people must be exploited by a small group which stands to gain by the change and is willing

where, as in the early internationalist days of Communism, projection is confined to a class enemy, it is difficult to re-interpret Marxist revolutionary ideas in any terms which coincide with modern anthropological work. Any fundamental change in the pattern of a culture depends upon changes in the character-structure of its members, both as cause and as effect. It has been repeatedly shown that such changes depend less upon public and political institutions than upon relatively inconspicuous environmental forces in childhood. It would be perfectly possible to make a case that the changes in a given culture which might follow a shift in the pattern of infant-feeding behaviour are likely to be more extensive than those arising from a revolution in the distribution of economic and political power.

This view does not suggest that economic change is impracticable, but only that it must be conducted within a different type of social change, and not merely affixed to an existing culture. The adversary of 'revolution' to-day is not human nature but the necessity for modifying cultural patterns as a whole by scientific means. No such modification can be brought about through the interplay of aggressions and projections which makes up almost the whole of traditional political thought, both governmental and revolutionary. *The status of power-mechanisms as a means of self-expression for delinquents and for aggressive impulses effectively limits their use as a means of social change based upon observational research.*

To this extent, modern sociology would seem to uphold the libertarian-anarchist rather than the totalitarian-institutional conception of social change, though it does so with marked reservations. Repudiation of authority may spring equally from maturity and immaturity, and in a proportion of agitators it is in itself a psychopathic trait. Yet the basic tenets of many of the earlier anarchist writers, fundamental human sociality, the inappropriateness of coercive means to

to furnish the necessary leadership and to use extreme methods to achieve its ends.'—W. F. Ogburn and M. F. Nimkoff, *Handbook of Social Psychology* (Kegan Paul, 1946).

modify cultural patterns, and the basing of political change upon the assumption of personal responsibility by individuals, through 'mutual aid' and 'direct action', retain general validity in terms of the new conception of sociology which does not depend on the unconscious forces which may have prompted those who stated them.

Anarchism, though it shows some of the actionistic fantasy that is common in the radical thought of the nineteenth century, is based not so much on a utopian future as on a return to a primitive naturalism which shall free men from the political state and economic exploitation. In this sense anarchism has much in common with the mythology of the return to an Arcadian past.*

The Golden Age, however, like the 'state of nature' has faded out of the currency of social thought, and the actionist fantasies with it. The profound transformation of the original myths of Godwin or Shelley through the systematic study of man has brought them more into line with the realities of experience. Like other myths, they are not programmes of action, but glimpses of possibilities, to be followed or rejected in terms of reality and experience. If there is or was a Golden Age, its existence is in the human mind rather than in concrete societies. To this extent, the myth of human sociality, like the myth of human health, is one of the aspirations which humanity has perpetually attempted to reconcile with reality, first by magic and by prayer, later by empirical action, and later still by planned investigation and applied science. Revolutions which give too great and too literal credit to their myths in the historical sense, and which aim at concrete retrogressions in society, by abandoning machinery and technical progress, are contradictions of the entire tendency of human values. If society fails to fit the known requirements of man, we can modify it in one direction only, towards increased control over ourselves and our environment. This type of revolution stands in sharp contrast to the policy of revolutionaries who wish to plunge forward

* Kimball Young, op. cit.

empirically, and revolutionaries who are obsessed with a largely illusory past.

A somewhat curious prescription has been suggested for 'our present discontent'. Unfortunately it is not based upon scientific aetiology but is a manifestation of psychopathology. Its plan is to scrap the whole modern industrial set-up and return to the pre-industrialized form of society. This was seriously put forward as a line of action some years ago by Gandhi in India, and also found favour in the Irish Free State. Life, however, is set in a one-dimensional time track. Neither in the individual nor in the group can it turn back, and in times of difficulty the impulse to regress may be attended by fantasy notions leading into even greater difficulty those who attempt to put them into practice.*

The mystical and regressive substitutes for the centralized state passed out of the currency of scientific thought with the end of the last century. The opponents of the institutional approach to-day are to this extent upon psychologically securer ground. In the words of a twentieth-century anarchist:

We are not a primitive society, and there is no need to become primitive in order to secure the essentials of democratic liberty. We want to retain all our scientific and industrial triumphs—electric power, machine tools, mass production and the rest. We do not propose to revert to the economy of the hand-loom and the plough. . . . The fundamental truth about economics is that the methods and instruments of production, freely used and fairly used, are capable of giving every human being a decent standard of living.†

Our criticism of centralization or of institutional society is not a proper ground for the rejection of the methods which have made our enquiry into it possible, but only for further efforts to select the favourable and eliminate the harmful in its fabric. The only serious prospect of de-industrialization lies in the catastrophic destruction of Western society by war, famine, or exhaustion, and such a revolution would restore government indefinitely to the jungle and the bacilli.

* Halliday, op. cit.
† Herbert Read, *To Hell with Culture*, 1943.

If the word 'anarchism', as a name for the attempt to effect changes away from the centralized and institutional towards the social and 'life-oriented' society, carries irrational implications, or suggests a preconceived ideology either of man or of society, we may hesitate to accept it. No branch of science can afford to ally itself with revolutionary fantasy, with emotionally determined ideas of human conduct, or with psychopathic attitudes. On the other hand suggested alternatives—'biotechnic civilization' (Mumford), 'para-primitive society' (G. R. Taylor)—have little advantage beyond their novelty, and acknowledge none of the debts which we owe to pioneers. 'Free society' is equally undesirable for its importation of an emotive and undefinable idea of freedom.

If, therefore, the intervention of sociology in modern affairs tends to propagate a form of anarchism, it is an anarchism based on observational research, which has little in common with the older revolutionary theory beside its objectives. It rests upon standards of scientific assessment to which the propagandist and actionist elements in nineteenth-century revolutionary thought are highly inimical. It is also experimental and tentative rather than dogmatic and Messianic. As a theory of revolution it recognizes the revolutionary process as one to which no further limit can be imposed—revolution of this kind is not a single act of redress or vengeance followed by a golden age, but a continuous human activity whose objectives recede as it progresses.

3: 2 *Incentive*

Centralized society has developed a theory of incentive at least as rigid as its theory of government. Industrialism in its early stages wrought such disorder in the existing pattern of life that its students may well have mistaken a highly abnormal for a typical state of affairs. Many of the presuppositions of our culture are traceable to the belief that no man will work without the sanction of poverty, exactly as its politics assume that no man will be sociable except under pressure.

Social incentives in various cultures are affected by too many elements, including crude physical factors such as climate, for generalization to be possible. Industrial society, lacking accurate data, provides only three main driving forces, profit, power, and fear, and a large number of its difficulties have arisen from these assumptions. Even in our own society to-day, profit unsupported by fear of destitution is not as potent a force as its theorists believed—acquisition is only practised for its own sake by obsessionals of the miser or collector type. The genuinely incentive elements in profit as a source of work and of delinquency are probably rather the status, security, or facilities which it gives than the immediate economic advantage. Power as an incentive we have already discussed. Fear is by far the most important cohesive force in modern centralized societies. It is the most convenient means of influencing conduct when common ground ceases to exist between the legislator and the public, and it can capitalize the confusion and aggression which make more positive approaches useless. Unfortunately it also aggravates the difficulties which the confusion and aggression create.

Fear, maintained by legislative and commercial groups as a main technique of persuasion, has already become our most important means of government. This is as true at the level of 'blood, tears and sweat' as at the level of body odour and constipation. Crowds, like bullocks, are most easily directed by loud noises. The modern citizen lives under a barrage of threats directed at his security, his independence, his sexual powers, and his desire to maintain a competitive status. This continual uproar blends with the inherent insecurity of asocial life, and with its phenomenal speed and congestion, to play a large part in the production of individual anxiety states, and in their counterpart, the chronic political, social or economic crisis. These newspaper crises are reflected statistically in the suicide and accident rate, and in the incidence of physical conditions such as perforated peptic ulcer. We have become too far acclimatized in the continuous noise, insecurity and movement of centralization to be fully aware of its effects, but these appear to include an observable sympathotonia, a continuous readiness for 'fight or flight' in the face of traffic, machinery, political speeches, wars, slumps and threats. Any temporary withdrawal of these stimuli leaves an unnatural quiet, like that which we notice when a clock stops.

The failure of the incentive-mechanism in industry has provoked a great deal of study. Russian communism, while fully exploiting fear and privilege as incentives, shows a better understanding of human behaviour by supplementing them with appeals to social status, the desire for approval and the competitive impulse. The difficulties which social democracy is encountering to-day are largely due to its neglect of basic human urges. The most significant positive incentives are probably emulation, expressed in dominance-patterns of proficiency rather than power, the enjoyment of creative occupation, the desire for social approval, and the attainment of a secure status. Financial incentives of the orthodox type having failed to reconcile individuals to the absence of such rewards, centralized governments find themselves driven to rely on straightforward coercion and conscription of labour. In this case again, the techniques of war-time government tend to become increasingly incorporated into peacetime life.

The problem of repetition work can only be overcome by a recognition of the facts and by a definite restatement of values. There is a case for accepting a reduction in the standard of physical amenities if we can obtain greater personal stability by doing so. Some at least of the unsatisfactory occupations could be eliminated by this means, others by a more determined application of technology. The extension of local responsibility, and of workers' control in industry, are also means of overcoming individual frustration. The main manufacture of a civilized social community is satisfactory individual life, and to this administrative norms, such as productivity, Great Power status and efficiency, are entirely secondary. Whether syndicalism, or the other types of economic solution offered by political theory, are answers to these problems can only be ascertained by experiment. The idea that human beings only work if forced to do so is a product of the system which rests on that assumption—it does not apply in the comradeship group, the primitive society, or the scientific research unit. No psychologist has yet determined the forms of external coercion, other than the coercion of the physical universe, which provided the incentives of Freud, Lister or Pasteur. It is the fate of our culture to make us underestimate ourselves.

3: 3 *Punishment*

Our negative incentives are of the same kind. The controversy which still rages over the means of dealing with delinquents turns on the efficacy and desirability of punishment, but punishment itself is more complex than the simple clout for disobedience and sugarstick for obedience which we tend traditionally to accept. In the first place, punishment may be deterrent, designed to inspire fear in others rather than reform in the delinquent: it may be reformative, a compulsory measure of psychotherapy: it may be retributive, and satisfy the impulses of society towards revenge and atonement. To this complication we have to add the fact that we now know that punishment may be actively desired, and may itself prove a source of satisfaction rather than of discomfort to the individual.

Since the advent of penal psychiatry, punishment as a means of dealing with delinquents has come to exist at two levels. On one hand we have the attempt to rationalize existing legal and administrative penal methods: on the other, the prisons and the courts as they are. The attempts to apply science to the prevention and cure of delinquency, so long as they are institutional and official attempts, have to be ingrafted on a system which assumes that social misconduct is the outcome of deliberate and malicious choice, and that such choice is best deterred or altered by confinement in the company of other delinquents, under conditions of squalor and idleness, and under a discipline designed to undermine self-respect and sociality. The enormous progress which has been made in some types of penal institution is always something added or affixed to this older pattern. Irrational and delinquent tendencies among the legislators, personal maladjustments giving rise to demands for bigger floggings and severer disciplines, perpetually hinder the attempts of the more progressive and better-informed penologists to make their ideas effective. The debates of the Houses upon the Death Penalty make depressing reading.

In fact, it is no longer possible to follow the conservative school of penologists, who take law and punishment at their face value as purposive mechanisms for suppressing delinquency, without turning a blind eye to an entire field of recent research. Precisely as there are grounds for suspecting that power is chiefly a mechanism for the discharge of aggression, there are reasons for inferring a widespread aggressive and unconscious motivation in penal law which makes nonsense of any attempt to treat its professed objects as real. Since Westermarck pointed out that no culture could regard its attitude to delinquency as rational until all primitive religion had been removed from its methods of dealing with violators, the face-value estimate of law and punishment in Western societies has become more and more dissonant with experimental and observational research.

The most cogent evidence for the rejection of punishment as a means of modifying conduct comes from the field experience gained in experiments with delinquents, normal and abnormal children, and even chronic recidivists who have exhausted the repertoire of legal penalties.* Work of this kind shows a striking unanimity of response in all these

* See W. D. Wills, *The Hawkspur Experiment*, Allen & Unwin, 1941; *Eliminating Punishment in the Residential Treatment of Troublesome Boys and Young Men*, Psychological and Social Series, 1946; and M. Paneth, *Branch Street*, Gollancz, 1945. See also references to Wehrli, Osborne, Kellerhals and several others in P. Riewald, op. cit.

groups to the type of social approach which is unindignant, unofficial, and based on the rehabilitation of positive social attitudes by the agency of what Christian theologians have termed charity, and what we may term human solidarity. This approach in no way implies a preference for the delinquent, or a neglect of the mischief he may do. It is, however, both empirically justified by a long tradition of human experience, which political theory has tended to despise, and theoretically justified by the knowledge of the mechanisms which form conduct. Sentimentalism, from which attempts at penal reform have not been immune, is in essence a concentration of feeling on the pleasurable sensations produced by an action or a belief rather than on its truth or appropriateness; these are condemnations which apply not only to over-tolerance, by reformers, of antisocial conduct, but to most of the policies of institutional punishment, which are eminently unfitted to their supposed objects.

No society, however utopian, is likely to remove altogether the causes of delinquency. We can, however, reject elements in society which we recognize as favouring them. The mechanism of restraint which operates most effectively is one which centralized institutional societies undermine— the interaction of public opinion and introjected social standards. The only case in which crime in this world brings inevitable consequences on the criminal is when it occurs in a social group from which there is no satisfactory escape, and in violation of universal standards. Our lack of experience of this force of public opinion in city aggregates makes us rather too ready to underestimate it. The ultimate sanctions of such a community, ostracism and excommunication, are probably more powerful than any form of institutional penalty. They may enforce restitution, expiation, or even banishment. How far these reactions in society are properly 'punishments' is a matter of terminology.

East (op. cit.) writes:

The armchair critic who opposes the retributive element in punishment sometimes seems to forget that it has a deep-seated biological significance. In a cultured society it may be necessary, and advantageous if it preserves a correct relationship between the turpitude of the offence and the severity of the award. . . .

It is perhaps fair to point to the large number of such critics in modern psychological literature: many of these have extensive personal experience of delinquents and of penal psychiatry. The crucial point seems to be the determination of the function which punishment is intended to perform if it is neither deterrent nor reformative. While we cannot underrate the importance of ritual acts in human life, the ritual character of retributive punishment certainly rouses a greater resistance in rational minds than the ideas of restitution or reform and deterrence. The origin of this resistance is in the vagueness of the purpose which is being served and in the patently emotional background of most advocacy for retribution. If it is the expression of solemn execration for antisocial behaviour, a case might possibly be made out for it, though it is difficult to see why such expression need take the forms which the law upholds as appropriate.

In spite of these arguments, there is undoubtedly a justified spirit of scepticism toward orthodox punishment abroad in modern psychiatric thought and literature which is bound to be reflected in the attempt to modify society. This scepticism certainly does not arise wholly, or even in a major degree, from a tendency to prefer the delinquent to society: some part of it may be due to overestimates of the place of mental disease in the causation of crime, but by far the greatest part comes from realization of the mechanisms by which cohesion is maintained in social societies, and the discovery in clinical experience that positive approaches to the child and to the adult delinquent offer a wider scope for attitude-changing. The main criticisms of punishment in the institutional pattern are its selectivity towards certain types of antisocial behaviour, its predominantly magical character, its inefficacy in statistical terms, its utterly unconstructive methods, and its use as a cheap substitute for the reconstruction of society. Even the attempts of centralized states to

develop a more constructive side to the penal system, intelligent as these occasionally are, involve real administrative
risks of stabilizing the prison population as a permanently
under-privileged group of cheap-labour-providers. Even the
most conservative penologists have come to regard punishment in general, and the blend of depersonalization, loneli-
ness, boredom and bullying which characterizes the prison in
particular, as last resorts, to be replaced by advice, treatment,
rehabilitation, or expedients such as probation, wherever
possible. Apart from the theory of punishment, its practice
in centralized communities shows so little regard for common sense or its professed intentions that defences of the
prison system in terms of modern knowledge are difficult to
take seriously. It is perhaps understandable that none of the
more enlightened members of the Prison Commission, however much time they may have spent as prison medical
officers or administrators, have any first-hand experience of
imprisonment 'from the receiving end'. East's references*
to the 'bland and easily assimilable' prison diet are a measure,
perhaps, of the separation of theory from fact.

In abandoning the conception of crime as something
chosen in cold blood by the criminal for its nuisance-value
to society, appropriate for eradication by punishment and
avoidance by moral stamina, we have to draw distinctions
between general aims and immediate policy. In full knowledge of the existence of bodies of contrary opinion, this
writer would take the view of Forel that one such objective
is the total replacement of punishment by positive social
attitudes and by the remodelling of society.† On the other
hand, if the general psychiatric distrust of punishment were to
lead to a general exodus of psychiatrists from the institutional prison service, both society and the criminal must suffer.
East,‡ apart from his conspicuous contribution to what we

* East, op. cit.
† 'There is to-day an unequivocal answer to the question: What can be
substituted for aggression in criminal law? Non-violence and selfgovern-
ment as means of education.' (P. Reiwald, op. cit.).
‡ East, op. cit.

know of delinquency, has done valuable service in bringing home to us the difficulties of the harassed official on whose doorstep criminals are deposited, not in the hypothetical future, but daily at the present time. It is to the pressure of psychiatrists who are in actual contact with the mechanisms of the law, as well as to those outside the system, that we owe such experiments in positive social rehabilitation as have been undertaken.

The reform of penology and the modification of society are complementary, and each will appeal to different personalities as a chosen field of activity: we cannot separate the two, or we find ourselves rehabilitating delinquents without having any normal society in which they can express the attitudes we teach. It is an interesting fact that more experimental 'social' groups have so far been created in the process of treating delinquency than in the context of daily life.

3: 4 *Planning in Social Terms*

A study which criticizes existing ways of life provokes a very reasonable demand in the reader for alternatives at least as concrete as the criticisms. If such a book contains nothing like a party programme, it will certainly disappoint some people. It should, however, be clear that the fundamental criticism of modern society is its lack of organic growth, and the absence of scope for normal human biology and initiative. To follow this kind of analysis with a detailed institutional programme would be illogical. Sociology points to the ways in which human beings can achieve secure and satisfactory attitudes, but a condition of this kind of stability is the ability of individuals and groups to create their own institutions without too much pressure from outside. We can obviously discuss desirable patterns of industry, economics, and political life, but the forms which actually arise out of a social conception of society will depend on experiment, national and local temperament and conditions and the objects which particular communities have in view.

Detailed individual studies have appeared, and will no doubt continue to appear.*

In so far as we have distinct suggestions to offer, they are means of realizing the conditions for this kind of experiment. The only programme which can be put forward with confidence involves:

(1) Measures to increase public awareness of the state of society and of the results of research into human social psychology. The focus here is educational, through the explanation of the mechanics of specific problems such as war or social neurosis, through the training of specialist psychologists, sociologists and physicians, and a particularly determined attempt to make modern ideas felt among the educating groups—teachers, lecturers, students, town planners, writers, etc. Even institutional politicians, though they are not the most promising material, can be reached in this way.

(2) Fundamental experiments in communal living and control of resources. These have a demonstration value out of all proportion to their size. They are often open to the criticism that they depend on the society which they are attacking, but it is hard to see why they should not do so. A widespread growth of spontaneous experiment of this kind is likely to prove a serious competitor to the less satisfactory institutional apparatus, and influence it as much as experimental rehabilitation has influenced penology. It is only in daily practice that the day-to-day problems can be worked out.

(3) Specific pressure, towards controlled break-up of large city aggregates, increased workers' control in industry, with decentralization of large units.

(4) Concentrated propaganda to introduce sociality into the place where character-formation takes place, the family and the school. The value of this type of instruction has been proved by the striking change in ideas of parental and educa-

* See G. R. Taylor, *Conditions of Happiness*, Bodley Head, 1949; L. Mumford, *The Condition of Man*, Secker & Warburg, 1944.

tional discipline during the last twenty years. The failures which encompass the modern family are to-day far more the product of institutions such as war and city life than of persisting parental ignorance and severity, although much clearly remains to be done. We run the risk of becoming involved in a circular process—child attitudes may be firmly fixed by the seventh or eighth year: the pressures of asocial life disorganize parents and homes, and in turn produce new supplies of handicapped future parents. The child can only be stabilized through the parent, and the parent is already adult.

While it is certainly easier to create sociality by nurture than to reconstruct adult attitudes, there is no ground for assuming that adults cannot be re-educated. The main problems of extending sensible and social childhood background arise from social factors such as housing, war, conscription, and insecurity. Part of the work of child guidance is therefore the focusing of adult attention on these hindrances, in the hope that a realization of what is involved may lead to effective action.

(5) Individual psychiatry. While treating the individual, we cannot let slip the opportunity to indicate to him the social as well as the personal causes of his illness. The task of adjustment is not the recreation of centralized morale and of acquiescence, but the building of a morale based on negative resistance to bad institutions and positive determination to experiment in social living so that they can be superseded. This is the most specifically revolutionary part of our work. It may involve not only individual therapy but such measures of propaganda as we can undertake through writing, speaking and living. It may involve specifically revolutionary activity, such as the encouragement of direct resistance to delinquent authority and the withdrawal of scientific support from projects involving secrecy, the suppression of information, and the abuse of technology for war purposes.

Direct pressure through the mechanism of parliamentary parties does not figure in this list of aims. There are those who will feel that such an omission is perverse. On the other hand, it is doubtful, on the grounds which have been set out in this book, whether progress through the institutional pattern is worth attempting, and whether a more revolutionary approach is not valuable in itself, as a means of bringing home our point. In all our contacts with the centralized pattern we run the risk of being incorporated into it, of becoming a veterinary department. This does not mean that social psychologists should withhold advice, or decline to participate in health services, but that they should be aware of the independent discipline of science and refuse to compromise it. Some activities of our society are so inimical to this discipline that we can hardly retain it in accepting them. Others, depending on our individual judgment, may seem worthwhile as palliatives. Medicine has always a specific duty to reduce human suffering, provided that it does not allow public health to become the passive acceptance of public disease.

3: 5 World Government

In the preface to this study, reference was made to the attempt of sociologists in UNESCO to employ the machinery of that body in promoting social studies. It was pointed out that attempts of this kind must inevitably raise new issues in the relationship between research and governmentally-sponsored bodies.

The claim made by the United Nations Organization, and by advocates of world authority, has been stated by West*.

Within their established societies men need externally administered law, not because their consciences are weak, but because their prejudices are strong, while outside their established societies men need externally administered law for both these reasons. . . . We can hardly repeat too often that order rests on force. The World Authority must always be able to concentrate at any point . . . force sufficient to repel with certainty any challenge to its order and authority.

* Ranyard West, *Psychology and World Order*, 1945.

It will be seen that the claims made for world government spring from, and are identical with, those made for national government, both in their assumptions and in their corollaries. The appeal of this type of argument to psychologists and sociologists is difficult to explain. Apart from the assumptions about the place of coercion in maintaining sociality, the evidence relating centralization to delinquent-selection in office should alone be sufficient to make us critical of any organization in which unprecedented power is vested in individuals drawn, not even from publics, as in the case of national states, but from a council of governments, among whose members psychopathic selective factors have already operated.

Some part of the appeal of such a thesis comes from the confusion in the minds of many scientific workers between the highly desirable central organization of resources by *ad hoc* bodies and the central exercise of power. A rather similar confusion existed in the early socialist movement, and was largely responsible for the failure to deal effectively with the growth of totalitarian patterns within the socialist ideology. Hard as it may be to accept the inevitable charges of nationalism which such a view must face, we can only accept the assumptions and policy of world government at the sacrifice of the whole body of evidence about the motivation of social conduct, and about the nature of centralized authority, which anthropology and social psychology have provided in the last half-century. The argument that such coercion as is involved in world government would be directed toward communities, rather than persons to whose conduct these discoveries apply, can properly be answered by asking how a community can be coerced without the coercion of its members. The United Nations has already shown itself hostile to attempts by peoples to 'go behind the backs' of their governments, and it is doubtful whether this reluctance springs wholly from questions of procedure.

It seems, in fact, as if the concept of institutional world government, for all its attraction to those who accept the self-estimate of the State in national society, is a direct inversion of the process which we require. We have suggested that the delinquencies of states arise at two levels—in the psychopathy of publics, and in the psychopathy of individuals expressing their own and their culture's aggression through the mechanism of power. The restraint which can effectively prevent delinquent action by states must be applied to the individuals who directly initiate policy, and to the subjects who support them. Such restraint can be applied at one level only, that of the individual, who by his withdrawal from delinquent attitudes undermines the social support they receive, and renders impotent the individuals whose policies are imposed upon society only through its acquiescence or its co-operation.

3: 6 *Conclusion*

It is with this conception that we can fittingly end an examination of delinquent patterns in human society. If we wish to find responsible and social attitudes, it is perhaps to the lives of individuals, in the broad current of their various containing cultures and prejudices, that we must look, rather than to the leaders who contain, or float on the surface of, those cultures. The impulse of sociality, distorted by many forms of unreason, and moulded by stress into many destructive and unwelcome patterns, is still the most clearly discernible thread in human cultures. The killings and the hatreds are consistently directed not at recognizable men, but at effigies set up by stereotypy and fear, and it is the scarecrow costume placed upon these other human individuals by psychopathic processes in the minds of their attackers which we are concerned to strip off, exposing the human flesh and the human face which underlies them. That flesh once seen and assimilated to our own, we share in a more conscious degree the species-solidarity exhibited by most social animals.

Man is appealed to, to be guided in his acts, not merely by love, which is always personal, or at best tribal, but by the perception of his one-ness with each human being. In the practice of mutual aid, which we can trace to the earliest beginnings of evolution, we thus find the positive and undoubted origin of our ethical conceptions; and we can affirm that in the ethical progress of man, mutual support, not mutual struggle, has had the leading part.

PETER KROPOTKIN

No attempt to alter society carries a historical certainty of success. Progress is not inevitable—it depends upon luck and effort. Those who are depressed by the weakness of the resources of reason in the face of centralized propaganda and public irrationality may be cheered by the thought that although a collapse of our culture through renewed war would put back scientific achievement by a century, if not more, science itself is increasingly indestructible. Tyrants execute persons or suppress teachings, and wars destroy equipment and facilities, but we have no historical record of either of these forces successfully suppressing knowledge or eradicating the idea of the scientific method. If our deductions in sociology are correct, its forces will continue to operate, and ultimately to be recognized, even if secretly, in societies which reject it. Where we are right, we have 'human nature' on our side. The fantasy revolutionist and the armchair progressive may need reminding that Ricketts and Prowaczek both lost their lives in the study of typhus, and that social attitudes are substantially more dangerous to handle than micro-organisms. Neither medicine nor sociology are likely, however, to be intimidated by the occupational risks they may run. The rewards of both are too concrete and the obligation to pursue them too obvious. The only state we need to fear is the state of acquiescence which turns bacteriology into biological warfare and social studies into an accessory of propaganda and enforcement. It is on our own reserves of sociality and responsibility as scientists that our resistance to this kind of diversion depends. To cultivate these qualities in others, we need to begin by exhibiting them ourselves.

In this objective of individual liberation, many strands are contained. We have criticized the incentives of asociality, its punishments, its conception of authority and government—we have also cited a small part of the evidence which relates the form of societies, and their free or coercive orientation, to patterns which exist in the family, and which are maintained by the mores of parent-child or interadult relationships within the reproductive orbit. Religious writers sometimes challenge the power of humanist systems to produce an incentive-mechanism as powerful in its results on personal life as the supernatural view of life. We may reasonably look for this mechanism within the human activities of love and home-making: these are the key determinants of cultural pattern, and the source of profound reserves of psychical energy in individuals which our own culture fails to utilize, and obstructs by its sexual, economic, and social orientation.

It may be a long time yet before the *work* of the majority of the people can be made to be a spontaneous, creative experience. Since the technological difficulties are less, *love* would seem to offer a field for an earlier and speedier development of spontaneity, of positive, individualized values, and inner freedom. As Fromm (1940)† says, the person who truly loves others also loves himself; he loves life. Thus he differs from the frustrated, destructive person who wishes to restrain others and to destroy their values while he denies and punishes himself also. He differs also from the person who dares not be himself, but to be only what is expected of him, and who forces others into the same conformity. . . . At this perilous state in the development of the democratic way of life, it may be that this part of it will save the whole.*

Social psychiatry builds up the family upon this basis of guilt-free and responsible love, at once sexual and personal: the coercive and the asocial elements, expressed to-day in authority and military delinquency, hinder and destroy it.

† E. Fromm, *The Fear of Freedom* (Kegan Paul, 1940).
* J. K. Folsom, *The Family and Democratic Society* (Routledge & Kegan Paul, 1949).

We may perhaps find here the point of division between the cultural elements we have called life-centred and power-centred. They are, at root, the impulse of love and spontaneity on one hand and the impulse of coercion, authority, and guilt on the other.

For Product Safety Concerns and Information please contact our EU
representative GPSR@taylorandfrancis.com
Taylor & Francis Verlag GmbH, Kaufingerstraße 24, 80331 München, Germany

www.ingramcontent.com/pod-product-compliance
Lightning Source LLC
Chambersburg PA
CBHW050525280326
41932CB00014B/2455